Marietta's Stories

Happy memories of Glen
Ellen the ideal dwelling
place
Sincerely
Marietta (Heffner)
Showalter

Great Bend, Kansas, c. 1900

GREAT BEND, KANS.   Bird's Eye view, Main St. and Forest Ave.

Above is a bird's eye view of Main Street and Forest Avenue in Great Bend, Kansas. In the distance, down Forest Avenue, is the steeple of the Methodist Episcopal Church, where the Younkin family attended services. By the early 1900s, Great Bend was called home by more than 1,000 people and supported some thirty-four businesses including eight merchandise stores, seven grocery stores, three hardware stores, two banks, three grain elevators, two flour mills, and a brickyard. Over the years, the city continued to grow as a regional trade and service center, and increased dramatically when oil was discovered in the 1930s. From 1930 to 1940, the town's population nearly doubled as some 3,000 oil wells began to produce in the surrounding area. (Data Source: *Biographical History of Barton County, Kansas,* 1912)

Marietta's Stories
From Kansas to California, Memories of My Life

Marietta Younkin Showalter

Rayve Productions
Windsor, California

Rayve Productions Inc.
Box 726, Windsor, CA 95492

Cover Design — Mary McEwen, Design Girl Graphics

Except where indicated otherwise, all photos are from the author's collection.

Library of Congress Cataloging-in-Publication Data
Showalter, Marietta, 1916-
Marietta's Stories : From Kansas to California, memories of my life / Marietta Younkin Showalter
p.   cm.
Includes bibliographical references and index.
ISBN 978-1-877810-95-4 (pbk. : alk. paper)
1. Showalter, Marietta Younkin, 1916---Anecdotes. 2. Women--United States--Biography--Anecdotes. 3. United States--Social life and customs--20th century--Anecdotes. I. Title.
CT275.S49167A3   2012
978.1'033092--dc23
[B]
                                                              2011046712

Printed in the United States of America

For my family —
past, present and future generations

Marietta Younkin's Family

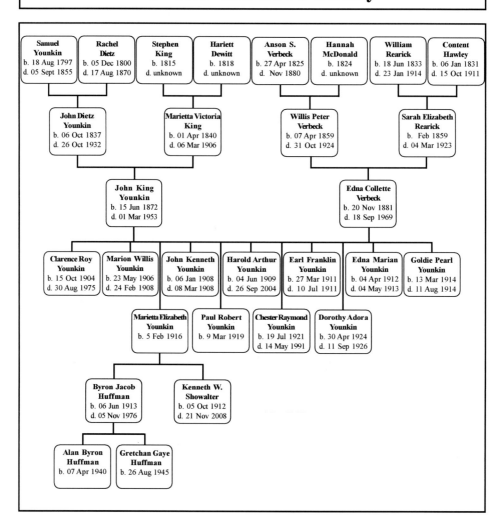

Samuel Younkin b. 18 Aug 1797 d. 05 Sept 1855	**Rachel Dietz** b. 05 Dec 1800 d. 17 Aug 1870	**Stephen King** b. 1815 d. unknown	**Hariett Dewitt** b. 1818 d. unknown	**Anson S. Verbeck** b. 27 Apr 1825 d. Nov 1880	**Hannah McDonald** b. 1824 d. unknown	**William Rearick** b. 18 Jun 1833 d. 23 Jan 1914	**Content Hawley** b. 06 Jan 1831 d. 15 Oct 1911

John Dietz Younkin b. 06 Oct 1837 d. 26 Oct 1932

Marietta Victoria King b. 01 Apr 1840 d. 06 Mar 1906

Willis Peter Verbeck b. 07 Apr 1859 d. 31 Oct 1924

Sarah Elizabeth Rearick b. Feb 1859 d. 04 Mar 1923

John King Younkin b. 15 Jun 1872 d. 01 Mar 1953

Edna Collette Verbeck b. 20 Nov 1881 d. 18 Sep 1969

Clarence Roy Younkin b. 15 Oct 1904 d. 30 Aug 1975	**Marion Willis Younkin** b. 23 May 1906 d. 24 Feb 1908	**John Kenneth Younkin** b. 06 Jan 1908 d. 08 Mar 1908	**Harold Arthur Younkin** b. 04 Jun 1909 d. 26 Sep 2004	**Earl Franklin Younkin** b. 27 Mar 1911 d. 10 Jul 1911	**Edna Marian Younkin** b. 04 Apr 1912 d. 04 May 1913	**Goldie Pearl Younkin** b. 13 Mar 1914 d. 11 Aug 1914

Marietta Elizabeth Younkin b. 5 Feb 1916

Paul Robert Younkin b. 9 Mar 1919

Chester Raymond Younkin b. 19 Jul 1921 d. 14 May 1991

Dorothy Adora Younkin b. 30 Apr 1924 d. 11 Sep 1926

Byron Jacob Huffman b. 06 Jun 1913 d. 05 Nov 1976

Kenneth W. Showalter b. 05 Oct 1912 d. 21 Nov 2008

Alan Byron Huffman b. 07 Apr 1940

Gretchan Gaye Huffman b. 26 Aug 1945

Marietta

1916   **2006**

CONTENTS

*"For I know the plans I have for you," says the Lord.
"They are plans for good and not for disaster,
to give you a future and a hope."*

Jeremiah 29:11

Younkin Family Gathering. This photo is believed to have been taken on the wedding day of the author's uncle, Clarence Lincoln Younkin, and his bride, Emma Parr Younkin, on July 9, 1886 in LaCrosse, Kansas. Family members are, seated in the front row, left to right, Harrison Riley, John Dietz Younkin, Adora Younkin, Marietta Victoria King Younkin, William Ellis Younkin, and Charles Younkin. Standing, left to right, are Anna Spencer Younkin, Samuel Younkin, Jennie Younkin Riley, John King Younkin (the author's father), Emma Parr Younkin, Clarence Lincoln Younkin, and Jennie Honderick Younkin.

ACKNOWLEDGMENTS

With deepest gratitude, I thank . . .

My parents, John and Edna Younkin, for nurturing and supporting me in accomplishing my life goals and helping me fulfill my dreams.

My son, Alan Huffman, who encouraged me to learn to use a computer, and is always available when I encounter technical problems. Alan is a tower of strength, helping me with many things.

My daughter, Gretchan Huffman McBurney, and my granddaughters, Heather Huffman Barnes and Laura McBurney Strom, for the many hours they spent editing and typing early versions of my stories and manuscript. These three women are special blessings to me.

John Dietz Younkin (1837-1932)

PROLOGUE

My Grandfather John Dietz Younkin, whose handwritten autobiography I inherited, inspired me to write my stories. Grandfather Younkin was born in Hamilton County, Ohio in the year 1837. He later relocated to Indiana, where in 1861 he married my grandmother Marietta Victoria King for whom I am named.

Not long after marrying Marietta, John Dietz Younkin enlisted in the army and served his country during the Civil War. In his autobiography, he gives a brief history of his life, relating many interesting incidents of his military service, describing his journey west with his young family and eventual settlement in Great Bend, Kansas. I enjoyed Grandfather Younkin's stories, and learned much from the details he provided.

For many years, beginning in local writing classes, I have enjoyed writing about my own life. After I had compiled dozens of stories, which writing class students and family members enjoyed, I began to think about publishing my memories, and was encouraged to do so.

Grandfather Younkin's autobiography is one of my greatest treasures, and it is my sincere hope that sharing my memories and photos in this book will bring insights about my life as I have lived it from 1916 to the present, and, more generally, about life in America during that era.

I sincerely hope readers enjoy my stories as much as I have enjoyed writing them!

Marietta Younkin Huffman Showalter

Wedding Day, December 28, 1903. *Shown above, my parents, John King Younkin and Edna C. Verbeck Younkin, pose for a formal portrait on their wedding day in Hoisington, Kansas.*

CHAPTER ONE

1916 — 1934
FAMILY & FAITH

The place of my beginning was Great Bend, Kansas on Saturday, February 5, 1916. My parents were John King Younkin, born June 15, 1872 in Indiana, and Edna Collette (Verbeck) Younkin, born November 20, 1881 in Kansas.

My father's parents were John Dietz Younkin, born October 6, 1837 in Cincinnati, Ohio, and Marietta Victoria King, born April 1, 1840 in New York.

My mother's parents were Willis Peter Verbeck, born April 7, 1859 in Wisconsin, and Sarah Elizabeth (Rearick) Verbeck, born in February 1859 in New York.

I feel blessed to have been named after my two grandmothers — Marietta, my father's mother, and Elizabeth, my mother's mother.

Maternal Great-Grandparents

My maternal great-grandfather Anson S. Verbeck was born on April 27, 1825 in Windham, Pennsylvania and his wife, Hannah (McDonald) Verbeck, arrived in 1824. The location of her birth is uncertain.

Marietta Younkin, 1916. *I was the eighth of eleven children born to my parents.*

My other maternal great-grandparents were born in New York: William Rearick on June 18, 1833; Content (Hawley) Rearick on January 6, 1831.

Paternal Great Grandparents

My paternal great-grandparents drew their first breath of life in Turkeyfoot, Pennsylvania: Samuel Younkin, on August 18, 1797; and Rachel (Dietz) Younkin, on December 5, 1800.

My other paternal great-grandparents were born in New York: Stephen King, in 1815; Hariett (Dewitt) King, in 1818.

Westward-Bound Ancestors

As the nation grew, my ancestors joined the westward movement. My paternal great-grandparents Stephen and Hariett (Dewitt) King were living in New York when my grandmother Marietta Victoria King was born in 1840. Later, the Kings moved to Indiana, where Marietta attended Purdue University and taught school.

Grandmother Marietta King Younkin and Beauty, c. 1893. *The cat shown above, known as "Uno" and "Beauty," was a family favorite. He was found 1891 by John King Younkin and his nephew John Elbert "Bertie" Younkin (son of Clarence Lincoln Younkin), while plowing on their Rush County, Kansas farm. Beauty earned his keep by catching rats and mice and he lived more than fifteen years, dying exactly one week after my grandmother Marietta King Younkin was buried in 1906.*

My other paternal great-grandparents, Samuel Younkin and Rachel Dietz, married in Pennsylvania and then moved to Ohio, where my grandfather John Dietz Younkin was born in 1837. Later, the Samuel Younkin family also moved to Indiana. There, John Dietz Younkin and Marietta King met and were married in 1861. They soon sought greener pastures in Battleground, Indiana, where John built a log house and their seven children were born. One of those children was my father, John King Younkin, born in 1872.

On the maternal side of the family, my great-grandparents Anson and Hannah (McDonald) Verbeck were among the early settlers in the Wisconsin Territory, where Anson and Hannah were married in 1846. Their union is recorded as the first solemnized marriage in Washington and Ozaukee Counties. Anson and Hannah's son, my grandfather Willis Peter Verbeck, was born in Wisconsin in 1859. He migrated to Kansas in 1877.

Sometime after 1870, my other maternal great-grandparents, William and Content (Hawley) Rearick, migrated from New York to Kansas. In 1880, their daughter Sarah Rearick married Willis Peter Verbeck in Kansas. One of their children was my mother, Edna Verbeck, born in 1881.

During the late 1800s in Indiana, my grandfather John Dietz Younkin assembled what belongings he could fit into a wagon drawn by a team of mules and took his daughter, my Aunt Jennie, and one son, my Uncle Sam, and headed to Kansas. Two sons had preceded them and were already settled. Grandmother Marietta Younkin and the three younger children — one probably being my father, John King Younkin, who would have been thirteen or younger — would later follow by rail. Grandfather Younkin filed a claim on 160 acres of land in Rush County, Kansas and built a sod house where the family lived until 1893, at which point they moved to Great Bend, Kansas.

At last, the scene was set for the birth of my generation in Kansas.

My Parents' Marriage

In the early 1900s, my father, John K. Younkin, taught school in the rural areas of Barton County, Kansas, its county seat being Great Bend. His work was generally in one-room schools, and his only means of transportation was by horse and buggy, occasionally by rail, depending upon the distance and location of the school to be reached.

Around this time, while seeking work in a new school district, my father was interviewed by school board members, one of whom was William Rearick. Now, Mr. Rearick and his wife, Content, happened to have a charming granddaughter, Edna Verbeck, who was employed as their housekeeper, and it wasn't long before John Younkin met Edna and fell head over heels in love. He

Proud Big Brothers. *Shown above, my brother Harold, right, is unhappy because he wanted to hold me, and Clarence is gloating because he got to.*

wasted no time courting her and soon asked for her hand in marriage. They were wed on December 28, 1903 in Hoisington, Kansas.

After a few years, John and Edna Younkin settled on a ten-acre plot of land at the edge of Great Bend. It was here that I was born, the eighth child of eleven children. In all, I had seven brothers and three sisters, but only four of my brothers — Clarence, Paul, Harold and Chester — and I lived to adulthood. My brothers and I were aware that six of our brothers and sisters had died, a fact that we accepted as part of the fabric of life. Many families lost loved ones in those days, and our parents reassured us that our deceased siblings — some infants, some older — were with God in heaven, and we found peace in that.

Only Clarence, my eldest brother and the firstborn of our parents, was able to remember all but two of our brothers and sisters. All of us were born at home, as were most babies in that era, and we were normal and healthy, but in those days before proper sanitation, refrigeration, antibiotics, and other health improvements, many children died. I can hardly imagine the awful heartbreak my father and mother endured. Yet, they expressed no bitterness, and their faith in God never wavered.

An Early Journey

The substance of this story was, for the most part, supplied by my mother, since I was a mere two years of age when it took place. The only recollection that I have of the event is fleeting but vivid: an image of me crawling over a bed in the back of a wagon. The year was 1918, probably summer.

Here, Kitty Kitty. *Even at fourteen months of age, I loved cats ... and I still do.*

My maternal grandparents Willis and Sarah Verbeck were living in Hoisington, Kansas, ten miles north of Great Bend, my family's hometown. Like most people at that time, Grandma and Grandpa were of modest, perhaps even meager, means. When news came that free government land was available in western Kansas for settlement, Grandfather Verbeck seized the opportunity for what he believed would be a better life, and he began preparations to move.

He had a wagon and a team of mules, and not much else. The wagon had a cover like those of pioneer days. It was a typical long-distance travel vehicle of the time, what we now call a recreational vehicle. En route, cooking was done over an open fire alongside the wagon, as was heating water for washing dishes, clothes and family members. Miscellaneous belongings were packed in the bed of the wagon, then a mattress

Yum! *I'm one and a half in this snapshot, enjoying a slice of Mother's delicious homemade bread.*

and bedding were placed on top for sleeping. The automobile had been invented only a few years earlier, so very few people owned one.

This journey would be a major undertaking for my grandparents, so it was decided that my mother and my two brothers, thirteen-year-old Clarence and Harold, just eight, would go along to perhaps be of some assistance. And, of course, I was included in the entourage. My mother wouldn't have thought of leaving me, even had it been possible.

No one told me how many days it took to reach our destination, which was Syracuse, Kansas, a small town on the Santa Fe railway only a few miles from the Colorado state line. This part of the state is mostly flat prairie land, its chief inhabitants at the time prairie dogs, rabbits and wild birds. Mother's sister Gladys Verbeck Buhrle and family lived in Syracuse, where Gladys' husband, Charles, was a railroad employee. The plans were for my grandparents to remain at their home while arrangements were made to procure land and

Cat's Cradle, 1919. *Above, I'm three years old, trying to master the cat's cradle string game.*

Sweet Siblings, c. 1922. *Although I longed to have a sister, my younger brother Paul and I had great fun together.*

construct a dwelling. This would be a house composed of blocks of sod cut from the prairie floor. This type of housing was used by early settlers and pioneers, there being little money and few resources. Some years later I saw a picture of this little sod house. What a dismal view it presented — not a single tree nor bush in sight, only sky and endless flat prairie.

After a short visit with Aunt Gladys and Uncle Charles, Mother and we three children headed home on the Santa Fe railroad. It was my very first train ride, and I don't remember a thing about it, because, Mother said, I slept most of the way home.

Age of Innocence

My parents encouraged us to live life fully, and the 1920s were years of total abandon for me — no worries, not a care in the world. My parents were wonderful — Dad, very affectionate and demonstrative; Mother, loving but more reserved. Their world was not carefree, but we children didn't know that. Looking back, I am sure that they, to the best of their ability, simply protected my brothers and me from the hardships and grief which they endured during those times.

In addition to their family, Mom and Dad cared for others. Anyone in need of help knew my dad would never turn his back on them, and I think my mother fed every hobo who came through the country. There were many of them in those days. We wondered if they had somehow or other put a mark of some kind on our place, which hobos were known to do. Or perhaps they got a whiff of Mama's bread as it baked — an average of three delicious loaves per day, three days a week.

We had few material things, so we valued what we had. Every Christmas I received a new doll until I was nine or ten years old, and Paul and Chet each got a toy car, and every year or two a new wagon which they shared. A carom game board and some card games rounded out our lists.

We spent many hours playing Rook, Flinch, Old Maid and Dominoes, and probably a few other games I have forgotten. These were our indoor activities, interspersed with various other events, such as weddings and church meetings. I vividly remember Paul pretending he was a pastor preaching a sermon, waving his arms and pounding the table, while Chet and I responded with "amen. . . amen   . . amen." We also had plenty of books to read, an activity Dad enthusiastically promoted. When I was very young, I enjoyed *Tom Thumb*, *The Gingerbread Boy* and *Black Beauty*.

Summertime was wonderful. We had a huge yard to play in, and just across the road from our house was a sand pit that Dad owned a half interest in. What a marvelous world for children that was! Where sand had been removed for commercial purposes, small pools had been created where we swam or fished. Cottonwood trees grew in the area providing shade, and we spent many happy hours there.

When a Penny Was Worth a Cent

I still pick up a penny from the sidewalk, but these days I ask myself why bother? It's such a long distance down, and the return is painful, to say the least — so little gain. It's a frugal habit that remains in my psyche.

When I was a very young child, I was given a small china piggy bank in which to save my pennies. I was taught that for every ten cents I received, from whatever source, I should put one penny, if not more, in the Sunday School collection, and an equal amount in the piggy bank. Now, at that time a penny could buy an all-day sucker, a short ride on a merry-go-round, or a half pound of watermelon. Even better, a penny could buy three pieces or more of malted milk balls, candy corn, or chocolate babies. I have to confess that I wasn't always willing or able to resist temptation. On more than one occasion the whole dime was blown away for candy.

My father was a rural mail carrier at that time. Each morning before leaving the post office to deliver the mail on his forty-mile route, he purchased, with personal funds, an ample supply of postage stamps for the convenience of his patrons. That was when you could mail a letter for three cents, and a postal card for one cent.

After finishing his route and his time at the post office, Dad usually came home with a pocketful of pennies. Being a generous and doting parent, the pennies were divided between my two little brothers, Paul and Chet, and me. I always deposited a few of my pennies into my little piggy bank. I think Paul and Chet saved theirs only until they could to get to a candy store.

One day when I was in the first grade, I asked my mother if I could take some of my pennies to school. I had in mind the little store across the street from the school where candy and gum were sold. Mother didn't think it such a good idea, but she gave in to my pleading and tied up several pennies in a handkerchief, which I put in the pocket of my dress, and off I went to school.

Our seating arrangement that particular morning was in rows of little chairs. I was in the first row as the teacher, Miss Dahm, read a story to the class, and all was quiet as she had the rapt attention of everyone. Everyone, that is, except me. To all outward appearances I was engrossed in listening, but my mind drifted to lunchtime and that candy store as I fondled the little bundle of pennies in my pocket. The hankie must not have been knotted, or my pocket didn't hold, for they suddenly came spilling out onto the floor with a clatter. I was mortified, feeling all eyes on me and knowing I had caused a disturbance. Before I could retrieve all of the pennies, Miss Dahm was down on the floor picking them up and mumbling something about not bringing money to school. She took them back to her desk, saying she would keep them until school was out. She then resumed reading the story. I was so embarrassed that I didn't have the courage to go to her desk after school and ask for my pennies. However, she came to me and gently and lovingly returned my pennies, suggesting that I not bring money to school in the future.

When class ended and everyone was leaving, I quickly regained my composure and headed directly to the little candy store where I spent my pennies on some licorice sticks and gumdrops, then headed for home. My indiscretion was soon forgotten.

Old Methodist Church, Great Bend, Kansas. *This church was constructed in 1886, dedicated in 1887, and was in use until 1924. My family and I attended services here as well as at the new Methodist Church that replaced this structure.* (photo courtesy First Methodist Church, Great Bend, Kansas, Archives)

First Christmas Memory

"I will hold Christmas in my heart, and try to keep it all year through."

Charles Dickens

The first Christmas that I can remember was when I was four years old. I can still picture in memory the little Methodist Church on the corner of Forest Avenue and Morphy Street in Great Bend, Kansas. A huge new church, just a few blocks to the east of the existing one, was under construction and not yet ready for occupation.

The Christmas Eve service was a very important part of the season for my family and an event we eagerly anticipated. That memorable Christmas Eve was clear and cold, but there was no snow on the ground. Daddy drove the family to the church, our little group consisting of Dad, Mother, my brothers, Harold, ten years old, and Paul, a toddler, and, of course, myself. I cannot remember my eldest brother, Clarence, who was fifteen, being with us.

Our car was a Model T Ford, vintage probably 1920, known as a touring car, having no windows that rolled up or down. There was no heater in the car so when traveling in cold or inclement weather, isinglass curtains covered the windows. The curtains, which were optional features on touring cars, had fasteners that snapped into matching holders in the car. Even with the curtains in place, it was still cold, so we usually bundled up with extra scarves, mittens and lap robes and took the weather in stride.

The church, aglow with light and the delicious fragrance of pine needles from the huge decorated tree standing at the front of the sanctuary, welcomed worshipers into its warm comfort. The program began with the singing of Christmas carols, followed by a pageant presented by children from the Sunday School. With utmost reverence, and only a few glitches, they portrayed the story of Christ's birth.

When the program ended, around nine o'clock, all of the children gathered around a huge decorated tree, anxiously looking forward to what came next, for we were certain treats of candy would appear. We were not disappointed! Presently, the back door of the stage opened and in bounded Santa Claus carrying a bag filled with treats. He beckoned all of the children to the front of the church and gave each of us a bag of Christmas candy and an orange.

Now, at that time oranges were not plentiful in Kansas, and they were quite expensive, so we appreciated that orange every bit as much as the candy. I remember taking it home and eating it bit by bit, savoring every delicious bite.

When we got home we were hustled off to bed so that Mother and Father could play their Santa Claus role. It was hard to go to sleep with the exciting anticipation of Christmas morning. Before slumber overtook me, I heard from somewhere a very faint cry which sounded like "mama." Oh! Could that possibly be a baby doll for me? I told no one what I'd heard for fear the spell might be broken, but drifted into dreamland with happy thoughts dancing in my head and visions of Santa leaving toys under the Christmas tree.

When morning came I was the first to race to the living room, and sure enough, under the tree there was a beautiful baby doll! What joy! There was a toy car and a game for Paul; and games, puzzles and books for Harold and Clarence. We were very happy and satisfied with Santa's gifts.

We had no fireplace with a mantle for hanging stockings, only a potbellied stove which warmed our house, so our stockings were "hung with care" on doorknobs or a chair back and oh, the joy of seeing them bulging with treats on Christmas morning. As I recall, protruding from the top of each stocking was a large candy cane, an orange, ribbon candy, and crayons or small puzzles, possibly some walnuts.

I believe our Christmas tree had real candles on it, for our house had no electricity yet. Mother lit the candles for only a short time, but the magic of Christmas lingered as we eagerly awaited the hour when she would serve the special dinner always prepared for the occasion. The sumptuous meal ended with suet pudding, a tradition handed down from my great-grandmother Sarah Rearick Verbeck. To this day, I continue the tradition, making the old-fashioned suet pudding that our family savors. Over the years, I have often had great difficulty finding two key ingredients — the suet and a certain type of raisins that most enhance the pudding — but it's worth the effort.

Let There Be Light

In the early 1920s the light in our small home was provided by coal oil lamps. The glass chimneys of these lamps required frequent cleaning and polishing, a housekeeping chore which generally fell to Mother.

At some point during this era, Dad arranged to have electricity brought in, which required getting the house wired. What grand and glorious developments we experienced from then on. In December our Christmas tree took on a bit of glamour, adorned with a string of colored lights powered by electricity.

In the days immediately preceding Christmas, my brothers and I were put to work stringing popcorn and cranberries into long festoons for decorating the tree. The bright red cranberries and white popcorn in their respective festoons were artfully draped around and over the tree's branches, making a colorful display, with hardly a need of further embellishment. However, Mother had numerous ornaments, some with special significance, others acquired through the years, all of them fragile and exquisite. These were all hung on the tree, giving it a final burst of splendor. Our Christmas trees were magnificent to behold.

My First Gingerbread Man

When I was five and a kindergarten student, our teacher had a little party for the class at Christmas. The one thing that vividly stands out in my memory is the gingerbread cookie she gave each of us. This was the first gingerbread man I'd ever had. My mother was always so busy she seldom baked cookies, and I had no grandmother nearby to do that loving task, so I was delighted with my gingerbread man. I decided not to eat the cookie until I could take it home and share it with Mother. The party ended, the class was dismissed and I started the long trek home (a distance of about a mile) with the gingerbread cookie clutched in my hand.

Marietta Younkin, age 10.
Mother managed my curly hair by braiding it.

When I was about halfway home the wonderful fragrance coming from that cookie was just too tempting, so I decided I'd take a little nibble, not enough to spoil the shape of the gingerbread man. However, it was so delicious I couldn't resist one more little bite. And then, much to my dismay, I dropped my wonderful treat on the sidewalk and it broke into several pieces. I was heartbroken not to be able to show my mother the gingerbread man intact. But not being one to give up easily, I gathered the precious pieces off the sidewalk and ate all but one small piece which I took home to my mother. She heard my sad story and promised that one day she would make some gingerbread cookies.

Courthouse Caroling

When I was still in grade school, we sang Christmas carols each year on the steps of the courthouse in my hometown of Great Bend, Kansas. My school, Washington School, was on the west side of town and the other grade school was on the east side. The week that Christmas vacation started, the combined schools met on a designated night and all the pupils filled several flights of steps of the courthouse in the town center. There, our voices rang out with all of the grand old Christmas carols. It was an exhilarating experience to be a part of that chorus on those cold, crisp nights, and it is a memory I treasure of those times when life was much simpler.

The wonderful gift the world was given two thousand years ago truly makes Christmastime the most wonderful time of the year.

Let the Music Begin

The new Methodist Church was the largest church in town, and it had a pipe organ I loved. It was a huge organ with rows of pipes, from the very large ones, which were the deepest tones, to the very small ones, the high notes. Every Sunday as I sat with my parents, I was simply enthralled when the organist began the prelude, and every hymn or piece of music that followed was a pure delight to my ears.

In later years I had the opportunity to attend a theater which also had a large organ. The music from that instrument transported me to heights unknown, and I dreamed that I might be able to play one of these wonderful instruments some day. I took piano lessons during my growing-up years, which somewhat fulfilled my musical aspirations. I practiced diligently and became a skilled pianist, which proved to be rewarding in many ways on many occasions. However, I still longed to play the organ, but I figured that wish was unattainable. Little did I know that many years later my pipe organ dream would come true.

Family Pets

My family has always had an empathy for animals. Each of my four brothers had a dog during his growing up years, and I had a cat. When one pet disappeared or died, it was soon replaced by another like animal. No one ever paid money for a dog or cat in those days. There were always people who had more animals than they wanted and were glad to give the creatures to anyone willing to take them.

At no time were there ever more than two dogs in our household, and our animals were seldom allowed inside our house, because it was small, and our parents believed it unhealthy to have animals and children in close proximity. But our pets were not neglected in any manner. Comfortable beds were made for them in one or more of the outbuildings, and they ate well. Canned cat and dog food had not come into grocery stores yet, and we probably could not have afforded it anyway. However, my older brother Harold liked to hunt, and wild rabbits were plentiful in the country. So, with his rifle Harold kept our one or two dogs supplied with rabbit meat. In addition, there were usually scraps from the table, and always plenty of milk, which our dogs and cats enjoyed.

Most people didn't take their pets to veterinarians back then. If a community was lucky enough to have an animal clinic, the professional veterinarian's services were generally reserved for farm animals that provided food and income for the family. When sick or injured, household pets were usually treated at home.

The Pet Parade

Around 1926, when I was ten years of age, someone gave a puppy to my brothers and me. His heritage and age were uncertain, but he was cute and playful, as puppies usually are. Paul, who was seven, and Chet, five, named the pup "Spot," not a very classy name, but the boys thought it fit his appearance.

When December of that year arrived, one of the festivities of the season was a children's parade. By that time Spot had about reached maturity and was a good-sized dog. We three youngsters thought the parade sounded like fun and decided we'd like to be a part of it. I'd decorate my doll buggy and doll, Paul could lead Spot, and Chet would lead our little dog, Trixie. Prizes and candy were also inducements that tempted potential parade participants.

Now, neither of the dogs had ever been on a leash before, and we had never heard of dog obedience training. Our dogs were free spirits, never having been tethered to anyone or anything. Nevertheless, we didn't anticipate any problems. Dad took us in the car to where the parade formed on Main Street. Santa Claus would meet the parade a couple of blocks up the street in front of the courthouse. There, the parade would end with treats and prizes.

Spot took to the collar and leash like a veteran. Being the happy-go-lucky canine he was, he had a great time sniffing and excitedly barking at the other dogs. He seemed totally unconcerned about the few snarls he received in return.

When the parade started, Spot lurched off in high gear, eagerly excited to join the boisterous crowd of marchers. Paul gripped the leash, bravely attempting to maneuver his feet more or less in the line of march when, suddenly,

they came in contact with the pavement. Amid shouted epithets, dire threats and screams of delight from youngsters with their pets, Spot joyfully raced onward, towing Paul in his wake at the end of the leash. Miraculously, this duo finished among the parade entry winners.

Back at the beginning of the parade, the scenario differed most dramatically. Little Trixie had no intention of being led anywhere by anyone. She sat down and refused to move. Chet pulled and tugged, all the while

First Bicycle. c. 1928. My parents gave me a bicycle that I was to share with Paul and Chet. but Chet gave my "girls bike" a thumbs down.

becoming more frustrated. He angrily tried to pull Trixie out of a sitting position, but she had firmly braced both front legs and feet and would not budge. Dad had to bodily pick her up and place her in the car, then take a tearful little boy to Santa's stand to receive his bag of candy. After that experience, the boys lost all enthusiasm for future pet parades.

Interesting Characters

As members of the human race we are all created after the image of God, yet we also are all different in our own individual ways, some more so than others. The difference might be physical or mental, appearance or ability, or any number of other human characteristics. The more extreme the difference, the more likely one is apt to be dubbed a "character," and in a small town, where everyone knows most everyone else, characters are especially memorable.

My old home town had quite a few interesting characters, one of whom was Claude, the Popcorn Man. Claude was born with deformed arms, one being little more than six inches long. Still, he deftly operated his colorful little red and white popcorn machine, dispensing that wonderful buttery popcorn every day except Sunday. For five cents he filled a sack to nearly overflowing, at the same time offering a bit of friendly chitchat to every customer. His stand occupied that same spot on Main Street in front of the bank for many years. A few years ago on a trip back to Great Bend, I felt a sadness when I noted the void where Claude's popcorn wagon had stood.

Another colorful character was Fred Michaux, who was sort of an old-fashioned recycler. During the 1930s and '40s the only waste disposal the town had was either do it yourself by hauling garbage to the city or county dump or, if that wasn't possible, there was Fred Michaux with his ancient team and wagon. Fred made infrequent trips down the back alleys of town, gathering whatever happened to be available for pick up, be it garbage, old clothing, trash or any manner of other people's discards. His wife, Lucinda, accompanied him most of the time, and together they were a colorful pair. She was buxom of figure, and her costume was something to behold. I suspect she garnered the choicest articles from Fred's collections, and always there was a hat to complete the outfit which she wore with much aplomb.

Lucinda was a proud but happy-go-lucky woman. Being dirt-poor seemed to be the least of her worries. She greeted everyone with the most infectious smile and laugh, and a conversation with her could brighten one's whole day. Fred, on the other hand, was quiet with little to say. His skin was very black, his stature as slim as a rail, his movements slow. Neither he nor his ancient team of old nags were ever seen to move faster than a slow walk. Lucinda's skin was a warm brown and her eyes and smile sparkled with friendliness.

It was Lucinda who always paid the bills. I do not know if there was more than an electric light bill, but I rather doubt it since they seemed to exist on the barest of commodities. When Lucinda went into the Power and Light office to make her payment she sat down at the desk and proceeded to retrieve her money. The girls in the office were amazed at where she kept her cash. It was somewhere in her cleavage, but they marveled at the time she took rummaging in the area for it. But it was always the right amount, and Lucinda sorted it all out on the desk, all the while laughing and giggling with the clerks before going on her way. Fred was probably waiting for her with the wagon in the alley.

The Not-So-Roaring Twenties

The era was called the "Roaring Twenties" but I really don't know why — perhaps I was not old enough to hear the roar. For me, the 1920s were quiet and peaceful, the happiest and most carefree years of my life. I had a loving family, the most important asset of all. However, our family was changing. I still had four brothers — two older and two younger — who were not always easy to contend with, but the eldest, Clarence, was grown and married by the time I was starting school, so he was around only at family gatherings and parties. I remember him mostly for his teasing. The next one, Harold, seven years my senior, was the entrepreneur of the family, so he was usually off somewhere busy with some money-making enterprise. When very young he trapped gophers in our dad's alfalfa field and collected bounty, ten cents per pelt, at the county farm agency. That was an early environmental program. He was never without a project that could bring in some cash. Since he was the one with the money, he had a bicycle, skates and other things, including a pony, all of which he carefully guarded. These were all totally off limits to me and the younger brothers.

I enjoyed playing with Paul, who was three years younger than I, and Chester, known always as Chet, two years younger than Paul. We had few toys, but invented our own games and activities. In the summer it was such fun playing in the sand pit that our dad owned. It was a plot of land consisting of probably two acres, shaded in some areas by cottonwood trees. Sand was a marketable commodity in Great Bend, dug by shovel and hauled by wagons and horses to building sites or for road repair and maintenance. Asphalt had not come into common use yet. When several loads of sand were removed, water flowed from underground to create small ponds, several of which dotted the area. None were deeper than one or two feet and posed no great danger. Like Tom Sawyer and Huckleberry Finn, my brothers built a makeshift raft that we propelled with a pole but, unlike Tom and Huck, we couldn't keep our raft afloat. It was heavy and in the shallow water, it kept sinking. Every time it went under, a salamander or two came aboard, which always brought a screech from me. They were harmless little creatures, but I was afraid they'd bite my bare toes.

Another pond had fish in it, which Harold had planted, and it was great sport when we caught one or two with our stick fishing poles. This pond was also a swimming hole, and when I wasn't present, my brothers, along with the neighborhood boys, went skinny dipping. Mostly, they splashed about and dog-paddled, but I'm sure they imagined they were as great as Johnny Weissmuller.

In winter those same ponds froze and we had fun on the ice. I think we had one pair of ice skates which we took turns using. They were not shoe skates, so not one of us became proficient at ice skating. We didn't fret or complain about not having sports equipment for each of us. We appreciated and had fun with what we had. When friends joined us, we would build a bonfire and roast wieners and marshmallows and have a great time.

Our family had plenty of livestock on the small acreage where we lived. One or two cows provided all the milk, butter and cheese we could use, plus a little extra cream which my mother sold at the local creamery for what she called her "pin money." We always had a flock of chickens with baby chicks hatching regularly. Not many roosters were allowed to live to an old age; their fate became the roasting pan or a pot of noodles, and we had fried chicken often. The hens gave us plenty of eggs, and when a hen got too old to lay eggs she became a candidate for chicken stew with dumplings. My mother was a marvelous cook. Our dad loved to garden and liked to try everything that was advertised in the seed catalogues, so we grew up eating every vegetable he could manage to grow. We didn't have many material things, but we ate well.

A Wonderful Surprise

On April 30, 1924 a most wonderful event occurred. I was walking home from school and as I neared the house, I saw Aunt Jennie Riley in the distance coming toward me. When we met, she greeted me with a loving hug and then said, "You'd better hurry home. The doctor brought a surprise for you in his little black bag."

I ran the last block, my mind running even faster, wondering what the doctor could possibly have brought in his little black bag. I was only in second grade, and not at all knowledgeable in the ways of the 20th century. This was before Dr. Spock, television, and children's books that explain procreation.

I ran the rest of the way home and hurried into the house. There, I found my mother in bed, and by her side was a tiny baby. Mom greeted me with "Here's that baby sister you've been wishing we'd get for you."

Wonder of wonders! Just what I wanted, my joy knew no bounds. It didn't matter how she got there, she was what I'd wished for. She was christened Dorothy Adora Younkin, and, as her middle name suggests, we adored her.

With four brothers already, I needed a sister, and I looked forward to all the fun I would have with her in the years ahead. Sadly, my joy was short lived, for sweet Dorothy Adora succumbed to illness before her third birthday, on September 11, 1926. I was overwhelmed with grief at the loss of this precious loved one. Graciously, God didn't let me know then how many other beloved family members I would grieve for during my very long lifetime. That foreknowledge would have been unbearable.

Memorial Day

In 1865 President Abraham Lincoln designated May 30 as Decoration Day, a the day on which our nation would pay tribute to the Union soldiers who had perished in the Civil War. Eventually, the name was changed to Memorial Day and honored all those who had died in battle, but it was still Decoration Day when I was a child.

To me, Decoration Day was as important as Christmas Day. Our town always had a patriotic program, parade, band concert, and observances at the cemetery, and our family always participated in many ways.

I remember standing on Main Street with younger brothers Paul and Chet, eagerly awaiting the parade, proud because we knew Grandfather John Dietz Younkin would be among the first in the procession. He was a Civil War veteran and a member of Great Bend's veterans organization, the Grand Army of the Republic (GAR), Post No. 52. Parade participants assembled at the bridge over the Akansas River, at the south end of town, where a brief service honoring members of the Naval forces was held, casting floral wreaths upon the flowing water. Following taps by the bugler, the procession formed a line and, led by the American flag, proceeded up Main Street. At this time in the 1920s there were few Civil War veterans remaining, and it was with great reverence that we observed our grandfather in the car that led the parade.

Upon reaching the courthouse, the parade dispersed and further observances were held at the cemetery. However, this was not always the order of events. I remember one year when the entire program, minus the parade, was held at the Civil War Veterans' burial mound in the cemetery. Another year the program was nearby at the American Legion Circle, where veterans of many conflicts were buried.

The cemetery was a veritable garden, having been cleaned and decorated with all manner of fragrant flowers the day before. American flags were everywhere, waving in the breeze, filling us with a sense of patriotism and peace. With programs and observances concluded, families went their ways, joining aunts, uncles and cousins, some having traveled distances to be with us.

Easter Reflections

Although spring weather is often unsettled with some unwelcome cold spells, frosts, and chilling winds, those days of white fluffy clouds in azure blue skies and warm sunshine reassure me that new life is coming. Since early childhood I have reveled in the beauty and the renewal of life that the season brings, the glorious celebration of Easter crowning it all. I was taught from earliest childhood the true significance of Easter Sunday; that is, the resurrection of Christ, giving the world new life and redemption. For me, this concept was most deeply instilled through attendance in Sunday School and church. I also enjoyed all the other accoutrements of the season.

My younger brothers and I were privileged to have Easter egg hunts, but I don't remember ever having an Easter bunny. That probably cost too much. My older brother Harold, always anxious to help Mom, rose very early Easter morning and hid the eggs that she had colored the night before. Our yard was spacious with numerous shrubs, so we had fun hunting for the eggs. One year our little fox terrier, Trixie, also an early riser, must have seen Harold making the nests and filling them, for she was out before Paul, Chet and I started our search. We soon discovered her feasting on the eggs in one hidden nest. Luckily, there happened to be only three eggs in that nest. When all the eggs were accounted for, it was time to don our new clothes and be off to Sunday School and church.

For me, new clothes were a part of "life's renewal," because Easter meant new clothes for my brothers and me and, sometimes, for our parents. My parents could not afford to buy me a ready-made store-bought dress, but that didn't really matter, because my mother was a skilled seamstress who made all of my dresses and when time permitted, the boys' shirts. I was allowed to choose the style and pattern for my dresses and also the material. For my brothers, new suits were purchased from a Sears & Roebuck or Montgomery Ward catalogue, whichever offered the most affordable price. When knickers were fashionable, boys' suits presented quite a problem for my brothers. They hated the long stockings that were a necessary accessory to the knickers, but unlike their sister, they were not given a choice. After all, bib overalls were not appropriate for Sunday School.

One year when I was around ten years old my choice of material for my dress was a soft silky material — silk, I think — in a lovely shade of deep pink or rose. When my mother had finished sewing it according to the pattern I had chosen, she decided to add an extra bit of adornment. My eldest brother, Clarence, had recently married Marjorie "Margie" Baker, who was quite artistic. Margie liked to paint and was able to paint on fabric, so at Mother's request, my new sister-in-law eagerly demonstrated her artistry. Together, they designed a pattern and my Easter dress that year turned out to be a custom design! Was I proud? You bet! I went to Sunday School feeling like a princess!

Easter Sunrise Service

I love Easter! Some critics of the season point out that it is a pagan holiday dating back to ancient times when festivities honoring the goddess of fertility included an Easter bunny and colored eggs. While those elements may be based on old, non-Christian traditions, Easter is a holy time in my heart. Since I am a believer in Christ, I love and celebrate on Easter Sunday because it is the day set aside by Christians in remembrance of the resurrection of Jesus Christ. Many people are drawn to worship services at Easter, and families traditionally get together to celebrate.

When I was a child, many churches held sunrise services, which were inspirational and memorable. One of the most dramatic pageants depicted the resurrection of Christ. The site for this performance was in the small village of Pawnee Rock, Kansas, only a few miles from my hometown, Great Bend. The little town is situated at the foot of a very high hill with outcroppings of huge rocks. For us flatlanders this was a mountain. When atop this hill one could see for miles in all directions the rich, totally level farmland surrounding it. The outcropping of boulders and rocks provided a scene very similar to pictures we had seen at church of the Jerusalem site where the crucifixion and resurrection of Christ took place.

The play began as the sun's first rays lit the sky. Atop the hill were three crosses. Farther down, nearer the outcroppings of the boulders and rocks, the actors and commentator gave an impressive portrayal of Christ's resurrection. The entire performance ended with a triumphal hymn of praise just as the sun made its full appearance in the early morning sky. More than a half century has passed since I witnessed that awe-inspiring event, but it is forever etched in my memory.

May Day Disappointment

Spring was my favorite season of the year, and it was especially nice in 1926. First, because school would soon be ending, I looked forward to being free of the long underwear and long cotton stockings. Then, there would be the last-day-of-school picnic or party! But before these last wonderful days, there were May Day festivities, always exciting rites to be observed in the spring.

We eagerly looked forward to the Maypole dance. Those in charge of the program would set up a tall pole which had many-colored streamers attached around the top. The children who had been chosen to perform the Maypole dance then took their places, alternating directions around the pole and grasping a colored streamer. When the music began, they danced or skipped in time to the music around the pole, weaving the contrasting colored streamers into a lovely design on the pole. The rest of us would sing and clap in time to the music.

That looked like such fun! How I would have liked to be one of those in that Maypole dance. But I was much too timid to volunteer, or in any way let it be known that I had such a desire. I was filled with fear, for I lacked confidence in my ability. If I were to make a wrong step, I might throw the whole party into confusion and end the Maypole dance. If I were to do that, my embarrassment would be devastating. I just couldn't take that chance.

Another spring activity that we enjoyed was the making of May baskets. In 1926, May Day was on a Saturday, so our teacher had us make our baskets on Friday, April 30, the last school day of the school week. This could be quite competitive as each child tried to make the prettiest basket. Miss Blender, our third grade teacher, gave each pupil colored construction paper and paste and after a few instructions, left us to create our baskets. I worked diligently to create what I thought was a very ornate basket. We were to fill the basket with flowers and hang it on the doorknob of someone we loved.

I knew exactly where I would hang my basket — on my Grandpa Younkin's door — but the basket would be for my Aunt Jennie Riley. She kept house for Grandpa, who, at the age of eighty-eight, was blind. I knew that Aunt Jennie would be the one to hear my knock, open the door and happily discover the lovely May basket filled with flowers. It would be a grand surprise! Aunt Jennie and Grandfather lived only about four blocks from my home, and it was on my way.

The day was warm and pleasant, and as I began the long trek homeward, I very carefully clutched my May basket. I looked for flowers along the way, mostly dandelions, but here and there a flower in someone's yard grew a bit too close to the sidewalk or the path I followed, and when temptation would overtake me, I'd add the posy to my basket. By the time I reached Grandpa's house I had what I thought was a fairly lovely bouquet in my basket.

I tiptoed to the door, hung my basket on the doorknob and knocked, then ran and hid behind a bush so that I could see Aunt Jennie's face when she opened the door. But alas, no one answered my knock. There was nothing but silence. What a letdown. With a sad heart, I walked the last few blocks to home. Not willing to risk another doorbell-ringing-and-hiding disappointment, I simply handed my May basket to Mother.

Time Out

When I was a child, we had no health insurance, but many people possessed medical books which gave advice on treating numerous childhood illnesses. My mother relied heavily on this source of information when we were growing up, so when my younger brother Paul

> **QUARANTINE**
> **SCARLET FEVER**
> **KEEP OUT**

came home from school one day feeling ill, she felt his forehead and knew that he had an elevated temperature. Having read from her medical book many times the symptoms of various ailments, she suspected that he showed indications of scarlet fever. During this era before antibiotics, scarlet fever was a major cause of death, and the disease was highly contagious, so Mom was naturally alarmed.

She called my father into the house and told him of her concerns, that she was going to call the doctor, and advised him to take the rest of the family and leave. My three remaining brothers, my dad, and I lost no time gathering a few things and moving to Grandfather Younkin's house. When the doctor arrived (they made house calls in those days), he examined Paul briefly and confirmed Mom's suspicion. Sure enough, Paul had scarlet fever. That called for a few extreme measures, the first being the placement of a big red sign tacked on the front of the house, with the word "Quarantine" emblazoned in large letters upon it. Paul was in the second grade at this time, about eight years of age, and he took a rather dim view of that big ominous red sign, for it meant that no one could enter or leave the house for the next three weeks.

The doctor left medicines for the duration of Paul's illness, along with instructions for his care, but now that Mom and Paul were virtual prisoners in the house, it was up to Dad to see that they received the necessary elements for survival. During Paul's confinement Dad delivered boxes of food to the door

Grandfather Younkin's Home. *When Paul contracted scarlet fever, my other three brothers, Dad, and I stayed here for three weeks. The house was located at 3322 West 17th Street, on the corner of 17th and Harrison Streets. Grandfather purchased it in 1892.*

and left them on the step. This seemed an interminable time for my brothers and me to be away from home. No doubt it was a lot more than that for our grandfather, forced as he was to house five extra persons for that period of time.

When the three-week quarantine ended, it was time to fumigate our home. Everything in the house had to be thoroughly saturated with a potent, foul-smelling disinfectant. Books had to be opened and stood on end with pages spread apart and left for several hours. When the air finally cleared and the house was declared safe for occupancy, we all had a happy reunion.

My Tonsorial Debut

The present state of the economy brings forth fear and trembling in many, especially among the younger generation who have never really known of the sacrifices that their parents made to obtain the necessities of life.

My parents taught us to be self-sufficient in many ways. One brother, Harold, who was six years my senior, became most adept at cutting hair. I believe he was about fourteen or fifteen at that time. I cannot recall on whom he first practiced to master his tonsorial skills but it was probably one of his gullible younger brothers. Certainly, there was never a thought of barber school or any professional training. Harold's tools were a pair of hand-operated hair clippers, a comb, and an old-fashioned straightedge razor with its strop. Soon, he became the family's barber, and, of course, the price was unbeatable. In those Depression Era days Harold wasn't paid, for no one had any money. People just did whatever they could to help one another, and during those tough times, Harold kept his younger brothers, his father, and Grandfather Younkin well groomed.

Occasionally, one or both of these youngsters, Paul or Chet, objected to having playtime interrupted for the ritual of hair trimming. Then, Harold the barber exerted his influence. Being older and naturally stronger, he practically tied the resistent culprit in the chair while he made him presentable. The young one found it futile to continue his objections, for Mom or Dad was always nearby to quell the disturbance and back up the barber. It was most important that we maintained the neatest appearance possible, and that meant taking advantage of whatever service was available when it was available. Harold was a very busy person, the entrepreneur of the family. This endeavor remained with him all of his life. Many years later during the time he served in the United States military, he was the barber for the men in his company.

I, too, have always been eager to learn a new craft or art form, and have found this to greatly enrich my life. I was around eleven or twelve years of age when I observed my brothers receiving their haircuts. I was fascinated by the ease of these performances and the results, and I felt quite confident that I could accomplish the same thing. All I needed was a comb and barber shears ... and I knew where they were kept. I wouldn't need the hand clippers.

Now, all I had to do was convince one of my younger brothers that he needed a haircut ... and that I could do it. Paul, who was usually a bit more willing than Chet to do my bidding, agreed to be my guinea pig. Where Mom was at that time, I don't remember, but Paul was soon draped with an old sheet and I was in business. The first snips were pretty easy, but then a few stairsteps began to appear, and the more I tried to even them up, the worse they became. Was I in trouble!! Facing the fact that once hair is cut there is no replacing it, I admitted defeat and prepared to take my punishment. Wonder of wonders, it wasn't the end of my world. Harold came to my rescue, skillfully evening out the stairsteps a bit. Paul, who ended up with the shortest haircut of his life, tried to avoid public appearances until his hair grew out ... and he also avoided me for a week or two.

A Rude Awakening

It was a cold day in November 1928. Snow had fallen a day or two earlier and hadn't melted because of the freezing temperature. Dad always got up very early in the morning and built a fire in the coal-fueled heating stove so that the house would be warm when the rest of the family got up. In

First Home. *I was born in this house and lived here with my family until the structure burned. That's Clarence on the right with his dog.*

the kitchen, besides the range, was a three-burner kerosene stove. Because it made heat in less time than the range, Dad always heated water on it to help start his car on freezing mornings. On this particular morning, he was heating water in a teakettle and another vessel filled to the brim. Then, he busied himself with other early morning tasks while the water heated.

While my brothers and I slept, Mother arose, dressed, and began preparations for breakfast. Suddenly, I was jolted awake by noise and confusion in the kitchen, followed by a scream from my mother. "Wake up and get out! The house is on fire!"

The water had boiled over on the kerosene stove and literally exploded in a ball of flame. Within a few seconds, grabbing whatever was in sight on our way out, we were all out in the yard, some of us in our bare feet and night clothes. I think I had a coat over my nightgown. I snatched a picture, of all things, off a table as I ran out the door. The picture was the only one we had of my little sister, Dorothy Adora, who had died in 1926. My two younger brothers, Chet and Paul, found clothes, maybe not their own but they were covered. My older brother Harold had awakened before we did, so he had his clothes on. He, Dad and Mom ran back into the house to save whatever they could. Mom was in the bedroom retrieving boxes of photographs and other things, which she passed to Harold through the bedroom window. My dad was in the living room pushing the piano to the front door.

Our situation was bleak. The fire department was called, but we lived over a mile from town, and the top speed for fire trucks at that time was only around fifty miles per hour. In addition, the nearest fire hydrant was blocks from our house, so we were on our own. Our nearest neighbors were in a Catholic convent, almost a block away, but their property bordered ours. They saw our house afire, and several of the resident nuns came running with fire extinguishers.

On a small portion of the convent's land, there was a barn and fenced lot that contained two or three cows and a flock of chickens. In charge of caring for these animals, as well as maintaining the convent grounds, was a large, husky black man with only one arm. When he saw our fire, he dashed to our rescue. The first thing he saw when he got to the front door was Dad struggling with the piano, and somehow, our one-armed neighbor managed to get hold of the piano, lift it out the door, and set it safely on the ground. We were amazed at his kindness and strength, and we never forgot the miracle, for that was what it had to be. By that time the house was totally engulfed in flames shooting skyward.

Paul, Chet and I were in shock as we stood in the snow watching in dismay as our home with all out possessions went up in flames. About that time the nuns appeared, approached Dad and offered to take us poor, woeful children to the convent for breakfast. Dad consented, but for some reason which I cannot explain, my brothers and I were a little fearful of the nuns. Possibly, it was because of the habits they wore; certainly they had given us no cause to be frightened. The boys clung to dad, no way were they going to leave him. I, however, went with those very sweet young women, though at the time I felt like a lamb being led to the slaughter.

The nuns were very gracious and kind to me, and soon all my fears and apprehension melted away. They brought me food and drink, and then went to look for some clothes for me. I don't remember that they found anything I could wear, except for a pair of shoes and stockings which they put on my feet. I thanked them for their kindness, and when Dad came to pick me up, he expressed his appreciation to them for their help and concern during our misfortune.

Our place of refuge at this time was my Grandfather Younkin's house, where Aunt Jennie made room for the family until Dad found a house to rent. He went back to work the next day, but we were not able to go to school until some clothes were rustled up for us. It was only days before Thanksgiving, so we didn't miss many days of school. News travels fast, and within a day or two, boxes of clothing and food came pouring in. The patrons on my dad's mail route sent or brought abundant supplies of food, including a turkey ready to roast for our Thanksgiving dinner, even cakes and pies and candy. Our friends and neighbors showered us with more good things. They even brought kitchen utensils,

pots and pans, and some furniture and bedding. Shortly after the Thanksgiving holiday, Dad learned of a house to rent, and with a few purchases to augment the things given to us, we were ready to settle in and go on about the business of living. Within those boxes of clothes and other things were several pairs of

St. Mary's Convent. *Before this building was a convent, it was Central Normal College, and my father studied there. When our home burned, nuns from St. Mary's helped us.*

shoes, and much to my delight, a pair that I could wear, albeit they were pumps with high heels. I would no longer have to wear the unattractive, black, old-lady shoes with laces that the nuns had given me. Oh, I had dreaded having to wear them to school and being different from everyone else.

In spite of the fiery crisis that struck our family, we were blessed by many people in numerous ways, and I have never forgotten the kindness and caring shown by the Great Bend community in our time of need.

Ol' Topsy

As far back as I can remember, there was Ol' Topsy. We didn't know her in her youth, so she was always known as Ol' Topsy. No one seemed to know her age, but her appearance showed that she was well advanced in years. Her hipbones stood out like mountain peaks, her ribs were clearly evident, and her backbone was visible from quite a distance. No amount of hay or other food, which was readily available to her, improved her appearance. However, she was a gentle old horse who served our family for many years.

It is not entirely clear to me, but from bits and pieces of information provided by my dad and my older brother, Ol' Topsy was acquired by way of a horse trader. It seems that in that era, when farming was done mainly with use of horses rather than machinery, there were in existence certain entrepreneurs whose business was to go about the country trading horses. They would approach a farmer, who perhaps wanted to be rid of a horse that he no longer needed or was too old to be useful and was not saleable at a stock sale. Because money was so scarce at that time, the farmer was usually willing to accept a small amount for the horse, rather than keeping it and wasting hard-earned cash on horse feed. Then, the horse trader, whose character may have been somewhat questionable, went about the country swapping one inferior animal for another, or selling them for a pittance. Thus, Ol' Topsy became a commodity of trade,

Marietta on Ol' Topsy, 1918. *Here I am at two years of age on Ol' Topsy's back. My father is holding me securely in place.*

my dad the recipient.

My father was not a farmer, but we did live on a place at the edge of town which consisted of ten acres. He was a teacher for many years, and later worked for the government as a rural letter carrier. In his time away from his regular job, he liked the small farming operations. This also helped sustain our family, which was not small. Part of the acreage was planted to alfalfa, which provided for the horses and the cow.

When it was time to cut the hay, Ol' Topsy was hitched to the mower along with our other horse, Dolly, and she faithfully plodded along. Later, she helped pull the hay wagon, hauling hay to the barn for storage. When Ol' Topsy wasn't doing farm duty, she occasionally was elected to serve in a recreational capacity. We couldn't afford a saddle, so we rode bareback.

I was not at all fond of riding bareback! Ol' Topsy's prominent backbone was not conducive to comfort. Also, she had a mind of her own and a very tough mouth. Once when she was giving me a ride, she decided she'd had enough of that activity and headed for the barn. I pulled on the reins with all my might, but to no avail. She would neither go in the direction I tried to guide her, nor would she halt so that I could get off her back. She had one goal in mind, the open barn door, and nothing was going to stop her. Now, the barn was actually more of a shed than anything else, with a low roof, and when Ol' Topsy reached the door, she entered without one moment's hesitation. I was focused on hanging on instead of ducking, so as Ol' Topsy raced into the barn, the low door beam peeled me right off her back, and I landed on the ground in a heap. I don't remember being hurt, except my pride, but I sought other sources of entertainment after that episode.

Ol' Topsy was our only means of transportation before Dad purchased an automobile. When a trip to the grocery store, church, or elsewhere was necessary, she was hitched to the buggy and dutifully trotted in the direction desired, then patiently waited while the mission was accomplished.

Our town of Great Bend hosted a yearly county fair that was held at the fairgrounds. The event was always eagerly anticipated by the community, and it was greatly enjoyed by everyone. One year during this time my Grandmother Verbeck and her daughter, my Aunt Gladys Buhrle, came for a visit with our family. When told about the fair, they both agreed that it would be a nice outing for Grandma. My mother was always busy with a baby or toddler, making it impossible for her to go, so she suggested that Aunt Gladys take Grandma to the fair. Dad would hitch Ol' Topsy to the buggy, and Aunt Gladys, who was familiar with the technique of handling the reins, would drive.

Ol' Topsy patiently waited while Grandma was helped and comfortably seated in the buggy, and Aunt Gladys got in and took the reins. Then, with a soft cluck and a slight slap of the reins on Ol' Topsy's rump, the horse nonchalantly trotted down the lane in the direction of the fairgrounds, which was quite a distance from our house. The two ladies were happily enjoying the ride and Ol' Topsy seemed blissfully contented as she trotted along. They had almost reached their destination when suddenly and without warning, Ol' Topsy decided she didn't want to go to the fair. Without further adieu, she made a U-turn in the middle of the road, and she was homeward bound. Aunt Gladys pulled with all her might on the reins and yelled "Whoa" at the top of her lungs, but Ol' Topsy had the toughest mouth in the world, and a deaf ear to "Whoa" or "Stop," so it was just "hang on, we're going home." The nearer she got to home, the faster she ran, and by the time she reached the lane in a cloud of dust, she had set a new speed record and demonstrated an unbelievable burst of energy. Poor Grandma, holding onto the buggy for dear life, thought she was a "goner" as they reached the lane and rounded

Third Grade Class, c. 1924, Washington School, Great Bend, Kansas. *This was the era of bobbed hair, but my father believed girls' hair should not be cut. So I, along with only one or two other girls in the entire school, endured long, old-fashioned tresses, mine usually in braids.* Students shown above are, from left row, front to back, Lester Bagley, Lucile Anderson, Mea Boil, Joe __, A.J. Brown, Mable Wilson; Second row, front to back, Ellen Terese Robinson, Dorothy Kennedy, Maxine Carr, Willie Keller, Ray __, Helen Bunzel, Thelma Rediger; Third row, front to back, Julia Pedigo, Hildegard Flure, Virginia Shay, Martha Kummer, Ernest Flure, Bertha ___. Fourth row, front to back, Ava Brown, Mildred Gallon, Marietta Younkin, Dorothy Flory, Mable Dun, Earl O'Connell. The teacher, standing at the back, is Mable Blender.

the corner on two wheels. Luckily, the gate to the corral was closed, so Ol' Topsy came to a screeching halt before she could reach the barn.

Dad heard the commotion and came running out to rescue the poor frantic ladies. When the dust had settled a bit, Grandma released the death grip she had on the buggy's arm and, pale and shaking, with hat askew, she was helped out of the buggy by Dad and firmly planted her feet on solid ground. It was then that she announced she never wanted to see that horse again, much less ride in a buggy behind her. And, Aunt Gladys found that her hands hadn't fused to the reins after all. She was just glad to be alive.

Musical Marietta, 1928. *When I was in the eighth grade I had the leading role in a school operetta, "Windmills of Holland."*

Grammar School Days

For every school year in my life there remains a memory that I can recall. Some are painful; others, quite pleasant. Growing up during the Great Depression was a time that is almost inconceivable for my grandchildren and great grandchildren. They cannot comprehend how little we had, nor how we could have been happy or content without television, rooms full of toys, a ride to wherever we happened to be going, cell phones, and electronic gadgets. Movies, too, were few and far between for us, even though the admission might be as little as a dime and never more than a quarter.

I vividly remember a very cold, wintry day when I was in the fourth grade. The ground was covered with snow as I headed to school that morning to walk the mile distance. I was bundled in a heavy coat with mittens and stocking cap, but on my feet, I had on only an extra pair of stockings and my everyday, over-the-ankle, hightop shoes because my parents couldn't afford boots or overshoes for their children.

About halfway to school my feet were so cold they began to hurt. I tried to run, thinking that would help the circulation, but it only made them hurt worse. A few more blocks, and I could hardly walk. It felt like I had sticks for legs. By the time I reached school, the bell had rung; I was late and sobbing from the pain. Miss Woods, my teacher, met me at the door, ready to reprimand me for being late, but when she saw that I could barely walk and noted my tears, her heart melted, and she led me to a seat in the warm room, very gently removed my shoes and massaged my icy feet back to life.

Another much more pleasant incident happened that same year. It happened during our time for art, one of my favorite subjects. Miss Woods gave each student a sheet of construction paper and told us to take our crayons and make a picture, the subject being something from our own imaginations. I remember drawing three trees and a small pond with a duck on it. I don't recall drawing the sun, but I made a shadow for each subject in the proper place and proportion, and that completed my picture. After the teacher had collected our artwork and scrutinized each one, she came back to my seat, laid a nickel on my desk, and announced to the class that my picture had won first prize. I don't know if it was those shadows on my picture that won her over, or if she just felt sorry for me, but I was thrilled beyond words to receive such recognition.

The Day the Circus Came to Town

What greater thrill is there than the circus? Especially when you are ten years old. Days in advance of that great event posters appeared all over town, as well as in the surrounding countryside, advertising the Ringling Brothers and Barnum & Bailey Circus, the "biggest show on earth." It always came to Great Bend. This was the county seat with the courthouse, and the hub, so to speak, of the community, where people living in smaller surrounding towns did the bulk of their business and shopping.

In the 1920s and '30s travel and commerce still moved mainly by rail, so Great Bend was served by three railroads, the Santa Fe being the main one, and it was by this means that the circus arrived very early in the day, usually before dawn. Many boys of the town, my brothers among them, were up at the first sound of the train's whistle. They hustled down to the depot, knowing there would be many tasks they might be hired to do in unloading and setting up the circus. It might be carrying water for the animals, or any number of other tasks to help the circus crew. For their efforts, they were given free tickets to the circus, a thrilling reward during those lean years.

There was a tract of land not far from the railroad tracks where the huge tent was set up and all the circus equipment as well. It was near the town's electrical plant, so it was convenient for their many hookups. The owner of this property kept the space available for the circus, and also for the carnivals that came to town during the summer months. No doubt it was very profitable to lease the site for the twenty-four hours the circus was in town, plus the week's stay for each carnival.

The big day finally arrived, officially beginning with the circus parade that was scheduled for 11:30 A.M. The only means of transportation for me at that time of day was my two legs. The family car was in use by my father, who was delivering mail on his rural route, so, Mother and I walked the mile and a half from our home to town. I love a parade, and since there were not too many in those days, it was important to see the circus parade. I danced with excitement when I heard the first notes of the calliope as it came steaming down Main Street at the head of the parade. The brightly colored wagons were beautiful, adorned with golden angels, birds and frescoes, and pulled by teams of huge handsome horses with fancy harnesses. There were also motor-powered vehicles driven by circus clowns, who were a good portion of the parade. Some vehicles carried wild animals; one, the circus band. I thought their lively music was grand. Then came the camels with riders in fancy costumes, and lastly, the many elephants, each grasping the tail of the one in front of him. As they marched around the town square and back to the circus ground, we happily awaited my father's return from his mail route so we could meet him and go see the circus performance. What a day in the life of a ten year old!

A New and Different Dance Step

A recent glimpse of a teen dance group brought forth a memory from long ago. I was a pre-teenager, I believe in the seventh grade, and I wasn't really into dancing yet. That would come later in high school.

My family lived at the edge of town on a small acreage. Our neighbors were within blocks of us, and all had property enough for gardens, yards, etc. Two of my girlfriends lived in the area. We walked together to school, that distance being little more than a mile, for we had no school buses. After school there always seemed to be time for play, especially in the fall before the days became short. One friend, Helen Bunzel, had among her treasures a Parcheesi game, so that's what we played at her house. Now, I can't imagine one of my grandchildren considering Parcheesi a fun activity, but I thought it was the greatest. Of course, television hadn't been invented yet, and except for football, there were no active games or sports outside of school.

My other close friend, Lily Bary, lived about half a mile from our house. Her home was similar to ours, with a garden, but their small fruit orchard was poorly cared for, and sheds and buildings were unpainted and dilapidated. Their house needed a coat of paint and probably some repairs, but times were hard, and I don't think her father had a steady job. Lily and I enjoyed spending time together, and it didn't seem important that her surroundings were meager.

One warm afternoon I had been allowed to go to Lily's house and while we were engrossed in a game, we suddenly heard a loud commotion coming from one of the buildings near the house. Tossing the game aside, we ran outside

The Old Swimming Hole, c. 1932

Skipping Rocks. *Pictured right, a friend skips a rock across the pond while I react with laughter to this unexpected candid snapshot.*

Fraternal Twins. Mary and Carrie Morgan relax in the sand.

Perfect Balance. *Mary Morgan supports my shoulders while I perform a balancing act.*

Bathing Beauties. Above, left to right, front row, Iris Binns, Opal Eldridge; back row, unidentified, Mary Morgan and Marietta Younkin.

to see what was happening. Lily heard her father yelling and stomping wildly about in the shed where her brother had a cage containing white rats. Lily's father had gone into the shed, looking for a tool, and stumbled against the rickety structure supporting the rats' cage, causing it to collapse. The cage door flew open, releasing the horde of rodents, and when Lily opened the shed door to see what the noise was all about, the scene was utter chaos — rats scampering in all directions and her dad yelling profanities and dancing about, for one or possibly more than one of those frightened creatures had scampered up a leg of his loose fitting overalls. Out the door he flew, performing contortions that were most amazing, cursing everything and everybody. The language I heard that day was not exactly suitable for one so young as I, so I hastily took leave of the scene and headed home. A few days later Lily told me that she had laughed at her father's bizarre dance, which had proved to be a disastrous mistake for her.

Junior High — Life was Just Sew-Sew

It is said that necessity is the mother of invention, and I have found that to be true in my life. In order to have some of the things I desired, such as clothes, I've had to make them myself. My mother made most of her clothes and almost everything that I wore when I was a child. Sometimes, she used salvageable material from discarded adult clothing, or sacks that flour was shipped in. She baked bread two or three times a week, so flour was bought in fifty-pound bags. The sacks made excellent dishtowels, also petticoats and bloomers for me, which all little girls wore under their dresses. One disadvantage of the flour sack was the colorful picture and name of the mill printed on it. Ours was the Barton County Mill, and the picture was the official state seal of Kansas, at least twelve inches in diameter, and quite colorfast. Household bleach had not yet come into use, so getting the color out of a flour sack was hard to do. More than one pair of my bloomers bore the Kansas state seal, however faint from countless launderings and time on the clothesline in the sun. But I was very modest and kept my underclothes covered at all times, carefully concealing the state seal. My dresses were usually made from pretty cotton prints. My mother would let me choose the material and she would sew the dress for me. The cost of the material was about twenty-five cents a yard, occasionally less.

In junior high, one class option for girls was home economics; for boys, there was manual training. In the seventh grade I learned sewing and in eighth grade, cooking, both of which I had eagerly anticipated. At the beginning of the year in sewing class we chose our pattern, a simple pair of pajamas. Each girl made the same kind of garment because it was a learning project. Anything more would have driven that teacher mad as she was a stickler for perfection.

If a seam was not straight, or if a notch didn't perfectly meet its matching notch, we had to rip open the seam and "do it right!" By the end of the school year I finally had a finished pair of pajamas, which I wore for several years. I also had a new motto. No, it was not "practice makes perfect." It was WHATSOEVER YE SHALL SEW, THAT ALSO SHALL YE RIP.

My seventh grade sewing experience did not entirely discourage me from trying again, only deterred me for a few years. When I entered high school, clothes were more important to me, so, with my mother's help, I again tackled the job of making my own dresses and enjoyed success in the process. Even so, I was limited on how much money I could spend on fabric, so I didn't have many dresses, but I was grateful for those I had. Joy of joys, I was treated to a store-bought dress when graduation time came.

Club Initiation

Who can understand the teenage mind, or find logic in teens' many antics, especially in the simple act of club initiations? As freshmen entering the new world of all-wise and powerful upperclass students in high school, we were allowed to choose an extracurricular activity or club. I thought the Pep Club sounded pretty good, so that was my choice. I knew that would ensure my attending the football games, among other things. Our games were held at night. It was always exciting to be in the stadium under the floodlights on a crisp autumn night.

Great Bend High School. *I enjoyed my studies and earned good grades in school but couldn't afford to go to college, so I went to work after graduating from high school in 1934.*

Great Bend Girls Baseball Team, c. 1933. Pictured above are, from left to right, front row, Ruth Cushing, Marietta Younkin, Clara Kummer, Virginia Trester, Lois Wilka; back row, left to right, Martha Kummer, unidentified woman, unidentified man, Hazel Hull, Dorothy O'Connell, unidentified woman, Audenchial Higgins, Evelyn Schroeder.

Another factor that I considered important was the outfit worn by Pep Club members. The school colors were red and black; the school's logo, the black panther. During those years our outfits had to serve more than one purpose or occasion. No cute pleated skirt and coordinated accessories to be worn only for special activities. Ours was an attractive bright red blouse with black tie, and a neat, conservative black jumper. At that time red was my favorite color, so I was right in my element. My mother made my outfit.

When the night of the initiation arrived, we poor, lowly, little greenhorn freshmen trembled in fear of what those mighty upperclassmen had in store for us. This could be a chance for those sophomores to get revenge for the way they were treated as freshmen.

I don't remember all of the silly things they put us through. They really weren't so bad, and we found we'd worried rather needlessly. But that, of course, was part of the fun — for them, at least. One final act did make a big impression on me, literally! I happened to be the last person in a line of a dozen or more girls, probably the smallest. We were all blindfolded and told to hold hands with the person next to us. Then the initiation leader led the line down the hall of the school's gym at a rather fast clip. She came to the end of the hall, and without sufficient warning to the unsuspecting initiates, proceeded to turn the corner. The first part of the string made it around the corner without much trouble and without slowing their pace. But you know what happens to the tip end of a whip. I didn't make it around the corner and hit that wall so hard I was out cold. So ended the initiation.

I carried that impression on my forehead for days. But, I could proudly say I was a member in good standing — when I had recovered enough to stand — of the Great Bend High School Pep Club.

Attitude Versus Diplomacy

When I was very young my parents taught me to be myself, and never to try to pretend to be something I could not live up to. "Just do your very best, whatever the task and the circumstances may be." I learned this lesson well, perhaps a little too well, for through the years I believed that if one showed pleasure or approval of something or someone that in reality was poor quality or distasteful, one was a hypocrite. Therefore, I was always forthright in expressing my opinions, and it wasn't until high school that I learned the benefits of a bit of diplomacy.

All through grade school I had made the highest grades and my name appeared on the honor roll at the end of each six-week period. When I reached high school I expected my academic successes to continue, but I soon learned that the adult world I was entering was very different.

High school introduced me to a new and more challenging teenage world. Most of my teachers were congenial, and I had no difficulty keeping my thoughts and opinions, which were sometimes critical, to myself. One science teacher was a slight fellow with dark curly hair, probably in his early thirties. Age being relative, I believed him to be well past middle age. My personal observation of him was an imagined one. During his lectures, he repeatedly ran his hand through his curly hair and each time he did this, I had mental visions of moths and other insects flying free. But I did well in this class, and I considered my mental pictures of him harmless. Another teacher, Miss Lowrey, who was sweet and kind, taught algebra. She had white hair and was quite elderly, I thought she had to be at least seventy five. Often during class she would fade while explaining a problem and doze for a few minutes. This usually elicited a few snickers, and sometimes a bit of mischief among the students. I didn't do quite as well in that class, whether her fault or mine ... no doubt mine.

Bookkeeping and shorthand classes were a horse of a different color. Both of these classes were taught by the same teacher — a tall, bony, hawk-faced man with slicked-back black hair, large horn-rimmed glasses, and an arrogant manner. His physical appearance I could tolerate, but his arrogant way of presenting himself before the class was something else. Each day before he began teaching, he always told a story or a joke he believed was clever or amusing ... and he expected everyone to laugh. I thought his stories were pointless and downright stupid, and I could not fake pleasure in hearing them. I am sure that my visage clearly revealed my innermost thoughts and feelings. This was a mistake! My negative attitude resulted in not receiving the high grades I wanted and deserved.

There were others in the class who shared my opinion of this teacher, but most of them were smart enough to laugh at his jokes. I'm not sure, but I believe I may have been the only student foolish enough to show my disgust; I was pretty naive in those days.

Eventually, several of us in the class put our heads together and hatched up a little scheme that we thought might take this egotistical character down a notch or two. This was also a mistake. One day during class, at a prearranged signal, we showered him with nuts — hundreds of them, from all directions. When the clamor died down, he indignantly stood up and demanded to know the name of the perpetrator of this little fiasco. He should have known better than to ask, because not one person gave him a clue; on the other hand, he probably had a fair idea. No penalty followed, neither did his teaching style change, except to add a sarcastic barb now and then aimed at us.

I passed both his classes, but with only a medium grade. I learned a lot of things that year, but perhaps the most important lesson was that it paid to laugh at this teacher's jokes. Most students who did received higher grades than I, for the same amount of work. It was my first lesson in diplomacy.

Depression Dilemma: High School Graduation, 1934

During the 1930s we went without a lot of things taken for granted today, including cars. Not every family owned a car and those who did usually had only one vehicle, which the father drove to work. Children today think, how could you possibly have had any fun?

Actually, we had a great deal of fun. The Golden Age of Radio began in the 1920s and lasted until the late 1940s, during which time most Americans regularly tuned in to broadcasts of comedy, soap opera, drama, mystery, children's shows, music of all kinds, religious programs, news, and more. This was also the era of the big bands and dancing was a popular entertainment. There were parties, concerts in the park, roller skating and ice skating in large indoor and outdoor rinks, sewing bees, and church potlucks. People also gathered to play games, sing, or enjoy the hometown band.

Jobs were scarce, and men with families were usually hired first. Even so, many family men couldn't find work. Many men — married and single — had to rely on government programs such as the PWA (Public Works Administration) or the CCC (Civilian Conservation Corps), which provided not only work for compensation but living accommodations in camps throughout the land. Young men in their teens readily joined the CCC to construct parks, bridges, and other projects.

I graduated from high school in 1934. Our class, with money so scarce, voted not to wear caps and gowns because of the rental cost, which was three dollars for each item. We agreed that we'd wear the best of what we already had. Since that year, seniors have always worn caps and gowns.

I had been saving my babysitting money for some time for a new dress for the occasion, so with a little help from my parents I found a very conservative dress with an irresistible price tag: $4.98. It was navy blue with a bit of white trim, and I wore it on many occasions after graduation.

The program concluded with the presentation of diplomas, bringing an end to twelve years of learning, and a beginning of new adventures. Some of us felt a slight "let down," there being no party to celebrate our graduation. There were no lavish parties nor excursions following graduation. Families honored their own graduates simply and in whatever manner they could afford. The idea of entitlement did not occur until some three generations later.

Twin Friends. *Two of my best pals were the Morgan twins — Mary, left, and Carrie, right. Our slacks were the latest style!*

Following graduation only a very few of my classmates went on to college. Those of us who were not able to pursue higher education obtained odd jobs wherever they could be found, even babysitting for twenty-five cents an hour. During high school I had opted for the commercial course, and eventually I went back to school and took a postgraduate course in business subjects. With that training, I obtained a secretarial position in an insurance and loan office. The salary was meager — six dollars per week — but with jobs being few and far between, I felt fortunate to have the job, whatever it lacked. Always, there was hope that things would improve in the future.

I gave half my salary to my grateful parents, and with my remaining three dollars, I was able to purchase my own clothes and other necessities. Three of my brothers were still living at home, and two of them, Paul and Chet, were in school. Back then, all family members helped as much as possible, because our survival depended on each person's cooperation and contributions.

In 1937 — still the Great Depression — our dad, having reached age sixty-five, was forced to retire from his job as a rural letter carrier. Yes, times were tough, but there was always a slim thread of hope that things were going to get better. It seems to me that, unlike today, as bad as the economy was during the 1930s, the average person did not harbor cynicism, lack of trust, and a feeling of betrayal by those in high government positions.

Life was hard, but not boring. Friends and families gathered for various social activities. Boyfriends who didn't always have funds for treating and entertaining sometimes shared transportation with others and played games or listened to records at the home of one of the gang. Yes, money was scarce and life was often hard, but we all survived ... and had a lot of fun in the process.

Babysitting Jack and Jill

During high school, and even for a time after I graduated, I felt fortunate to know one or two families who desired my services for babysitting. I was paid twenty-five cents an evening, not an hour. Often, there were dishes left for me to wash, and it was always part of the job to bathe and put the children to bed.

One family I considered to be well off. The husband was manager of one of the local grocery stores. His wife was a homemaker, as most women were in that time. They had two beautiful little children, a boy, Jack, and his little sister, Jill. I loved them both, and do not recall ever having trouble with them. But I could not say the same for their big ugly dog. He always barked at the wrong time or person. Once when he behaved rather badly, I threatened him with a broom I happened to be using at the time. This would have been of no consequence, but many days later I again babysat the youngsters. Their mother had picked me up in her car, and we all arrived at the door at the same time. Imagine my embarrassment when that stupid dog looked at me and cowered as though expecting a fatal blow. No one spoke a word. It would have been useless to try to explain that I had never hit him, only verbally threatened to use that broom on him. Anyway, there were no repercussions.

When I babysat past midnight I was paid a bit more, usually fifty cents, or possibly seventy-five cents if I had done the dinner dishes. One night, after putting the children to bed and doing the dishes, I was extremely tired, and when the couple failed to come home by 10 P.M., I decided to lie down and rest for a few minutes, not intending to fall asleep. Shortly after midnight they arrived home, the doors were locked and they had no key. They rang the doorbell, knocked, called my name a few times, and finally made their way into the house through a window. Through it all, their babysitter slept on. A few nudges and gentle shakes later I was surprised to learn I had fallen asleep.

My indiscretions in no way ruined my reputation, for it was not long until I again was called to babysit the same children.

The Mystery of a Tiny Treasure

Some time back I discovered a small ornamental object on a delicate chain among some old jewelry that belonged to my Mother. She has been gone for many years so, regretfully, I have no factual explanation as to how or where this little trinket came from. Therefore, much of my story will come from assumptions, observations, and experiences in my own life.

By way of explaining the keepsake, for that is what it is now, and was, as far as my Mother was concerned, the small object appears to be a bit of dentistry, or specifically, a baby tooth. I presume that it must have been the first tooth lost (by nature, in its proper time) by one of my brothers or sisters. It must have been one of my brothers' teeth, because my sisters died in infancy.

Knowing well my father's personality, what an affectionate and loving person he was, I am certain he treasured every happy milestone in the lives of his children. He, perhaps even more than Mother, enjoyed mementoes which brought to mind those happy occurrences. The sad occurrences, and there were many, were simply filed away in memory banks.

It is my assumption that this little treasure — a pearly baby-tooth necklace — dates back to my eldest brother Clarence's childhood, for he was the first child born to our parents. Dad considered the loss of the first tooth an important occasion, and the eldest son's baby tooth would have been especially memorable. So I feel certain that Clarence's little tooth was saved, taken to a jeweler who, per Dad's directions, mounted it in a setting and added a diamond chip, and attached it to a fine chain. Then, Dad lovingly presented the precious necklace to Mom, who treasured it for a lifetime.

If my theory on the origin of this necklace is correct, which I believe it is, this small treasure is more than one hundred years old.

CHAPTER TWO

1935 — 1945
ROMANCE & RELOCATION

In 1935 I met my future husband, Byron Huffman, who had just come home from a hitch in the army. He told me his enlistment and service had come about as a manner of survival, his family's circumstances being even less than ours. While in the army he learned a trade which would later prove profitable, but in 1935, with the country still in the Depression, jobs were scarce. Byron had taken whatever employment he could find — delivering groceries for a market, working part-time in a theater, and taking numerous other menial jobs.

Sweethearts. *I met Byron, the great love of my life, in 1935.*

We did not see each other often, the distance between our hometowns, Great Bend and Larned, being twenty-five miles. Byron had no car and although the Santa Fe railroad ran between our hometowns, my sweetheart couldn't afford a ticket. Nevertheless, he was determined to visit me, and true love always finds a way. Sometimes he hitchhiked and, occasionally, he rode the rails; that is, he jumped in freight cars at Larned for a free ride to Great Bend, provided, of course, that he could get on and off without being caught.

Economically speaking, things were looking a little brighter for our nation. With the help of President Roosevelt's "New Deal" and other government programs, a slow recovery began, many who had been unemployed were finding jobs, and businessmen were growing hopeful. Byron, too, was feeling optimistic, so he made a bold move and relocated to Great Bend where he felt there were more opportunities to find gainful employment because the town was considerably larger than Larned. Perhaps that was not the one and only reason for his move; he would also be closer to me. He was successful in his quest for work, and shortly was hired as a troubleshooter for Kansas Power & Light Company at the magnanimous salary of eighteen dollars per week. Still, it was steady work, and he looked forward to better times ahead, after the Depression.

Byron and I were beginning to make plans for our future, even though it would be some time before we'd see them completed. He received a promotion at work, which meant a slight raise in pay, and I, too, had gained another part-time job, so we were encouraged. I was able to save more than mere pennies — nickels and dimes, often more. And Byron was saving his spare change, too.

I began looking through bridal magazines for ideas, always with plans to make my wedding dress. My mother and I shopped for the material and soon were busy cutting, fitting and creating a thing of beauty for the most important occasion of my life. Mom was a very talented and efficient seamstress. She had made her own wedding dress, and had sewn clothes for me my entire life. Dad, too, had a few special plans of his own. The prospect of his only daughter leaving the nest saddened him more than he wanted to admit, but he had an idea which might keep the newlyweds nearby, if they chose to accept his offer.

Several years earlier, our family home had burned and had not been rebuilt. On the property, however, was a well-built garage that Dad thought

could be made into a cozy little cottage. He submitted the idea to Byron, who found it acceptable, and soon he was busy renovating the building. It had a room attached which had been used to store coal. That room, we decided, would be large enough for our kitchen, with a dining area at one end. When Byron finished cleaning out the coal dust and cobwebs, he built and installed some pretty cupboards, painted them white, papered one wall of the kitchen with a bright figured wallpaper, and covered the floor with shiny linoleum. It was now ready for the electric stove he had purchased earlier,

Byron's Favorite Photo. *Byron carried this photo of me in his wallet throughout his life.*

and a table and chairs. No one could have been more pleased nor more proud than I was of that little red and white kitchen ... even though it had no plumbing! We carried water from an outside pump.

The large room, which had once housed a car, needed only cleaning and painting, after which it would be ready for furnishing. This would be our living room as well as our bedroom. When we shopped for furniture we chose a living room set that consisted of an overstuffed chair and sofa, or hide-a-bed, and a chest of drawers. My youngest brother, Chester, had given us a lovely little table he had made in manual training, we called it a library table. I was so proud of it; and I still have it, seventy-six years later. My eldest brother, Clarence, gave us a large rug. My brother Harold's gift to us was an interesting picture, a fairly large, framed landscape, which, I thought, gave our living room a decorator look. Since the building contained no furnace or piped-in gas for heat, we went to a secondhand store and purchased a living room heating stove. It was comparable in design to the stoves of that time, but instead of burning gas as most of them did, this one used kerosene. Our room was complete.

I wonder if we or our clothes smelled of kerosene when we were away from home. No one ever indicated such. But there is an old saying that "Ignorance is bliss" ... and we were blissful — blissfully happy, that is.

The Engagement

Byron proposed to me in 1937, but I do not remember the exact date, nor his speech. But I do remember a time previous to this when we happened to be strolling together down Main Street in Great Bend, casually enjoying some window shopping. We paused a bit longer at the window of the local jewelry store. There were so many beautiful things on display, but amidst them all, we spotted a set of rings that seemed to call for our special attention. Since we both spied this set at the same time, we felt it was destiny that I choose my engagement and wedding ring. It would be several months before they'd be paid for, and I would wait until then to wear the engagement ring, but that didn't matter. Our commitment had been made. Since our desire was to have a spring wedding, we settled on a definite date — April 3, 1938.

Following protocol, my parents hosted an announcement party, and my closest friends were invited to our house for the event. Mom's decorations were simple but lovely, refreshments were delicious, and the engagement announcement was revealed in small party favors. Since Easter was near, the little favors were in keeping with the season, fancy Easter bonnets. At each guest's place was a little Easter hat, beneath which was a card with this message:

> *"We've been keeping this under our hat."*
> *Marietta & Byron — April 3rd, 1938*

Wedding Party. *My wedding day was the highlight of my young life.* Standing from left to right are the best man, Raymond Free, Byron and Marietta Huffman, and the matron of honor, Reta Phillips Willard.

Wedding Bells

Plans and preparations for our big day proceeded, regardless of the fact that no one had money to lavish on gifts, wedding or otherwise. I had been honored with a couple of showers — a kitchen shower by my best girlfriend, who would be my bridesmaid, and another by other friends. That would be quite sufficient to begin housekeeping. My beautiful homemade wedding dress cost in the neighborhood of ten dollars.

Came Sunday, April 3, 1938, our limited formal invitations to family and friends having been received, it was time to "get us to the church on time," as the lyrics to the well-known song goes. In keeping with our frugal budget, we had arranged with the pastor to perform the ceremony immediately following the regular Sunday morning church service. At the close of this service, the pastor requested that the congregation remain seated, and within minutes the organist began the wedding march. As I appeared on my father's arm and started down the long aisle, Dad totally forgot the little catch step that we had rehearsed and proceeded to guide me toward the altar with what felt to me like a quick step. I thought, "Good grief! Is he anxious to get rid of me?" But I promptly dismissed that idea. Poor Dad was just nervous. At the close of the ceremony we received congratulations from all two hundred-plus congregants as they left the service. Later, we boasted of having two hundred guests at our wedding.

Now that our vows had been solemnized at the altar of the Methodist Church, we would henceforth and forever be Mr. and Mrs. Byron J. Huffman. "Till Death Do Us Part" we had promised. Truly, we would fulfill that vow.

Ready for the Reception. *Byron's and my wedding reception was at my parents' house, where guests enjoyed a lovely buffet luncheon.*

Getaway Car. *Byron didn't own a car, so Dad loaned us his for our honeymoon. Byron and I didn't discover the "Just Married" sign and tin cans until we were well down the road.*

The Honeymoon

Our wedding reception was at my parents' home. Mom, in her usual efficient manner, had prepared a lovely buffet luncheon for our guests, assisted by my Aunt Gladys and, of course, my brothers. After the wedding cake was cut and served, toasts offered up, and congratulations heaped on us, I hurried off to change into my going-away clothes.

Now, my Dad felt bad that he had not been able to provide a more elaborate wedding for his only daughter, so a few days before the event he generously announced that we could borrow his car for a honeymoon trip. This was the nicest thing he could have done, since Byron had no car. (After we returned home, Dad often let us use his car, for we lived over a mile from town, which was quite a long walk, especially in stormy weather.)

In no time, amid a shower of rice and the happy shouts of well-wishers, we were off. Later, hearing the rattle of tin cans, we discovered about a dozen or more cans, individually tied with long cords to the back bumper of the car, the handiwork of my brothers, I'm certain. Undaunted, we drove on to our destination (minus the cans) to the city of Wichita, Kansas, 125 miles distant, where we had made reservation at a big hotel.

On the second day of our honeymoon when we faced the public for the first time as man and wife, Byron and I tried to act nonchalant, hoping no one would suspect we were newlyweds. HA! We didn't fool anyone! The valet who parked our car and did his customary cleanup swept out about a cup of rice.

Then we went to breakfast where we were again found out. Earlier, in dressing for the day, I had donned a new suit with a stylish cape that fastened at the neck with a clever little clasp. I felt so special in that suit and the cape was an elegant touch. Off we went to the hotel dining room, where we were shown to our table. I started to remove the cape before sitting down, but I could not get the clasp to open. How embarrassing. It had closed earlier without any trouble. Our waiter noticed my dilemma and graciously came to my rescue, opening the clasp practically with a wave of his hand, almost like magic. There was no use trying to act nonchalant any longer, anyone could tell we were greenhorns in brand new clothes. Byron and I finished our breakfast and when the valet brought our car, we headed out for parts unknown — it didn't really matter where — the scenery was new to us and we'd enjoy whatever came our way.

We were eastward bound, headed toward Missouri. Whenever a shop or a particular spot looked interesting to us, we stopped and investigated, once at a very pretty area alongside a stream where beautiful wild flowers bloomed profusely. Toward the end of each day we found a motel.

We meandered down through southeastern Kansas, enjoying perfect weather and scenery neither of us had seen before. We came to the small town of Columbus, and what a devastating sight! Buildings were badly damaged, some completely destroyed, and damaged trees were strewn everywhere. A day or two previously, a tornado had passed through this area and left a path of destruction in its wake. It was not a pretty sight, so we lost no time exiting the town, and drove on, crossing into Arkansas. Spring had preceded us. Everywhere we looked orchards were in full bloom, flowers and the fresh greenery of new leaves and grass with wonderful fragrance filled the air. We were in the foothills of the Ozark Mountains, and it was beautiful! Then, the sky became overcast and soon raindrops began to fall. So, we located a place to spend the night, a little rose-covered cottage which we thought was very romantic.

The change of weather convinced us that it was time to head back to Kansas. During the night the raindrops had turned into a steady downpour, the temperature was falling, and there we were in our spring clothes with no rain gear. As we headed north into Oklahoma the rain turned to snow, and we yearned to be in our own little home.

Filled with contentment, we counted our blessings. With the fifty dollars I had saved before our wedding, plus the little that Byron had managed to put away, we had been able to pay for our honeymoon. We had enjoyed a night in a first class hotel, eaten in a fine restaurant, traveled across two states, done a lot of sightseeing, and ended up in an Oklahoma snow storm. And after all this extravagance, luxury, and excitement, we had cash left over! When we reached home, we had enough money to purchase groceries for the following week.

A Slight Miscalculation

On April 7, 1940, Byron and I were delighted when I gave birth to our son, Alan. He was a beautiful, healthy baby, and we were typical proud parents. By December, Alan was eight months old, and we were looking forward to celebrating his first Christmas with my parents in their home, where we were living temporarily while Byron made arrangements to build our own home. A first Christmas is a memorable event in any young family's life, and we planned to have it properly recorded with many pictures, photography being just one of Byron's hobbies. He also liked working with wood, which proved profitable in many ways, especially at this time for our Christmas decorating plans.

My parents' house was very old, having being built in the 1800s, and lacked many things, among them a fireplace with a mantle. Our visions of Christmastime always included that scene — a fireplace with a mantle — as well as a brightly decorated tree. Since Mom and Dad had no fireplace, Byron decided to improvise and build one that would serve our purpose — for pictures at least — and would add holiday atmosphere to the living room.

There was no garage nor workshop, but the house did have a basement, used mostly for storing home-canned foods, and little else because space was limited to just one room. Access to the basement was from the kitchen through a door which lifted, basically a trap door in the floor with steps leading down. There was ample room down there for Byron's few woodworking tools and the materials he used to create various projects.

After taking a few measurements and deciding where to place our faux fireplace in the living room, Byron retired to the basement and went to work. This was not a project that could be completed in a matter of a few hours. Besides, he was a precise workman, finishing things to perfection. He spent several evenings on this project, finishing it with a brick-patterned covering, after which we had a very nice "fireplace." All he had to do now was to take it upstairs to the living room. Dad and I came down to assist him in moving it, and with all three of us tugging and pushing, we got it started up the steps. About three steps up, the top struck the opening into the basement and would go no farther, so we had to back down and try a new tactic. We tilted it, thinking a different angle might work, but that didn't get it up past the fourth step. There was just

Christmas Card Photo, 1940. *Byron built the mantle and snapped the photo of Alan which appeared on our Christmas cards.*

no way that thing was going to come out of the basement in one piece. Discouraged, we gave up and left the fireplace standing in the basement.

But this family doesn't give up easily. We had to change our plans for a decorated living room complete with fireplace, but not the pictures. With Byron carrying his camera and lights, and me carrying the baby, we headed to the basement where we took our Christmas photos. Alan's first Christmas, seated in front of the fireplace, was featured on the greeting cards we sent to family and friends that year, December 1940.

More Family Changes

Until the 1940s, our family had been a closely knit unit, my brothers and I living near our parents' home in Great Bend, two brothers, Harold and Chet, still living at home. The only member of the family who was no longer present at the many family get-togethers and special holidays which we enjoyed so much was Clarence. After marrying Margie Baker in 1925, he flew from the old family nest and moved to California. We missed him very much, but the very long distance between us was insurmountable. Travel was not easy at that time and extra cash for leisure trips was not in any family member's budget, so there was little hope of visiting Clarence.

Pearl Harbor and Beyond

My life in Great Bend had always been smooth and comfortable with only normal ups and downs, and I did not foresee any major changes in my future. But early on a Sunday morning, December 7, 1941 when the Japanese attacked Pearl Harbor, my carefree world disappeared. Life would never be the same again — not for me, not for anyone in America.

Are you old enough to remember where were you on that "infamous day in history"? I was busy in the kitchen of the little house Byron had recently finished building. The radio program I was listening to was suddenly interrupted with a news flash: "Pearl Harbor is being bombed by Japanese planes!"

Startling as this was to hear, I did not fully comprehend the enormity of such an event happening until Mom called a short time later to inquire if I was listening to the radio. When I answered in the affirmative, she said to me, "You know what this means, don't you?" I was still a bit dazed by the news, and by her question. You see, she had lived through World War I and well remembered the horrors, casualties and hardships of that time. No doubt she was also thinking of my three brothers who would likely be going off to war.

The day following the Japanese attack, December 8, President Roosevelt called the United States Congress into session and passed a formal declaration of war. Soon, we began hearing daily broadcasts of war updates. Within a short time, three of my brothers enlisted in the armed services. They were eager to serve, and by volunteering, or enlisting, they were able to choose the branch of service they preferred. Each week we read the lists of young men and women from our area who were leaving to serve their country and, soon, we grieved over casualty lists, thanking God when our sons and brothers were still safe.

Wartime Rationing

During the war, manufacturing plants were producing armaments and supplies needed for the war effort, and average citizens not serving in the military were expected to make sacrifices for those who were. Food, clothing and other daily necessities were needed by military personnel overseas, so commodities on the home front were in short supply. It was then that the government initiated rationing. We, like other Americans, applied for and were issued books containing coupons for gasoline and food items. You couldn't go far on the amount of gas you were allowed, and as for the food items, it took a bit of planning to stay within your limits of sugar, coffee, oleo, and other items, including meat. We almost forgot what bacon tasted like. The coupons were dated, so we were usually out of the item before time for a new issue of coupons was received. When you saw a line form somewhere, you knew it was for something scarce and hard to get, so you joined the line, never mind what it happened to be for. You'd find out when you reached the distribution point. Then, if it was something you didn't happen to need or want, you went about your business. It was worth a try. There arose many a slogan at that time, one of which I still remember: "Use it up, wear it out, make it do, or do without." The concept may have been new to some people, but it was the way I'd lived most of my life.

A Precious Time. c. 1942. *Before leaving for military service, my brother Paul, his wife, Annie, on the right, and I savor tender moments together.*

Empty Nest Syndrome

When my brothers enlisted in the Army, our parents were left with an empty nest, which was an unhappy situation. Byron, Alan and I lived only a few blocks from Mom and Dad, which was some consolation to them, but in the latter part of 1942 Byron was offered a position with the War Department in Omaha, Nebraska, which meant that we, too, would be departing from Great Bend. After many years of being surrounded by a good-sized family, Mom and Dad were desperately lonely.

It was then that Clarence, now divorced and remarried, invited our parents to spend the winter with him and his second wife, Cleo, at their home in southern California. Later, Mom and Dad got their own apartment, relocated to Los Angeles and made a new life for themselves. They enjoyed many more productive years, savoring sunshine and roses for the rest of their lives. At this point our family members were scattered across the United States, and we never again gathered together at one time as we had in bygone years.

Relocating to Omaha

Byron was eager to begin his new War Department job in Omaha, where his military training qualified him for a position as radio operator in the Communications Department. He was also an instructor for a period of time, teaching groups of Army recruits and Marines in radio communication. Everyone in the country was working in whatever capacity they were able to help in the war effort. We loved our country, and we knew we were going to win the war, whatever it took to accomplish that.

After Byron left to report for his new job, I packed our belongings, closed our house, and headed for Omaha with Alan. We traveled by train as we had no car. Even though it was not a great distance, approximately 400 miles, the trip was extremely uncomfortable. At that time the armed forces of our country were being transported from one place to another, and of course they were given priority over civilian travelers. The railroad cars were so crowded that some passengers were forced to sit on the floor in the aisles. Alan was only two years old, and I found it hard to be crammed into a small space in the back of the car, so we were glad when that journey ended.

Byron met us at the train station and we went to the room where he had been staying. He was exhausted and frustrated after struggling to find an apartment or house for us. The war industry was in high gear and there was a housing shortage due a large influx of people needed at the nearby army base. But Byron was a resourceful person, and although I do not know how he did it, he met a member of a family who was planning to leave Omaha for work in California,

Life in Omaha, Nebraska. *In 1943 Byron was working for the War Department in Omaha, and Alan and I enjoyed the city's parks and zoos.*

and an offer was made for us to occupy their house. They were friendly and congenial, and welcomed us. They told us we could move in immediately, as they would be leaving in the next two or three days.

We were delighted to have a house that was furnished. There was even a piano and a radio. We didn't mind the fact that it was six blocks from the nearest bus stop and that it was up a hill. However, three days later Mrs. and Mrs. Stuart, our landlords, were still with us, and we wondered why the delay. There was some conversation concerning an appointment, or car repair or something, but three more days passed with very little evidence of their leaving. By the end of the second week we thought we should look for another place to live. The house seemed a bit crowded now, and meals were beginning to be a problem also. The Stuarts always wanted us to eat with them, but their tastes were much different from ours, so Byron, Alan, and I ate out whenever we could do so without offending them. One day when we could get away, I took my little son and went window shopping, after which we met Byron at the end of his work day and ate in a restaurant. When we returned home and saw the Stuarts' car and trailer loaded and ready for travel, our spirits soared. At last we'd have some privacy! They said they would be leaving very early the next morning, so we fell asleep that night happy with the prospect of the new beginning we'd been hoping for.

Sometime after midnight but long before dawn, we were awakened by a lot of thumping and bumping and excited voices. What could be happening? We jumped out of bed, fearing the house might be on fire. We soon learned that the thumping and bumping noise had been made by Mr. Stuart as he bounded down the stairs from the bedroom. He had heard a noise outside and upon investigating, saw his car and trailer leaving the driveway, heading down the hill. Car thieves had hot-wired the ignition and were in the process of stealing the whole lot of it. There was one thing they were not aware of, however. The car had a lock that prevented the steering wheel from turning, so when the criminals reached the bottom of the hill, their ride ended. They made their getaway on foot, with Mr. Stuart in hot pursuit, but he was unable to catch them.

This event was most discouraging to all of us, but turned out to be less serious than appeared at the moment, and by the end of the day everything was settled. The Stuarts left early the next morning. A few days later they wrote to tell us they were happily settled in their new home in California and sent best wishes to us.

Since we had always lived in a small town, I was fascinated with life in the large city. There were many parks that could be reached by street car, as well as a good sized zoo, and of course the shops and department stores in the downtown heart of the city were a source of pleasure for me. During Byron's time away from work, we spent many hours in the different parks where Alan enjoyed the playground equipment, something we did not have at our Omaha home.

After about a year of work as a radio operator for the War Department, Byron was becoming so stressed that he felt he would have to seek a different job. I don't remember the exact process he went through, but he soon found new employment. I remember his coming home one day, elated to report that he had obtained a position as instructor of radio communications in a private school that had government contracts for specialized training for the armed forces. During the following year he instructed classes of both Army and Marine personnel in radio communications.

Around this same time we learned of an available apartment that was closer to the city and the street car line. It was also furnished, so we lost no time in making arrangements to rent it. The rent was thirty-five dollars a month. It was one of many in a complex of several buildings surrounding a very nice courtyard and a wonderful fenced playground. We were told that it had once been a very elite and exclusive residence, probably following World War I, but the intervening years had changed that, and during World War II we commoners were allowed to live there. All in all, we found it to be very satisfactory. Many families had children, so Alan had friends to play with on the wonderful playground, and I, too, enjoyed the friendship of many others who lived there.

By 1944 the government teaching contracts were drawing to a close, and we knew we'd soon need to make a change. The shipyards on the West Coast were in full swing building ships for the war, and were begging for more employees. We'd always wanted to live in California, so we made plans to seek our fortune there. With America's focus on doing whatever we could to end the war, Byron had no problem landing a job in one of the shipyards in Richmond. My parents were living in West Los Angeles, so we

Beloved Baby Girl, 1945. *My life-long dream was fulfilled when Gretchen was born.*

left Omaha and drove to their home, where Alan and I remained until Byron was able to find a place for us to live in Richmond. Government housing was plentiful there and it was only a matter of a short wait for an apartment.

When Byron was not at work, we enjoyed riding the electric interurban car and crossing the bay to San Francisco. Many times we went to Golden Gate Park for picnics. But the very best thing that happened in Richmond, California was the realization that we would be having an addition to our family. Just before that blessed event, the war ended and peace was declared. There was wild celebrating in San Francisco, as well as everywhere else. Then, on August 26, 1945, my lifelong dream was fulfilled when I gave birth to our daughter, Gretchan, and we had our very own celebration. With the war's conclusion, the shipyards also began shutting down, which meant the end of employment there. The time had arrived to move on to our next adventure.

Sewing Up a Storm

In 1940 when Alan was born, my sewing skills were put to good use. It was so much fun making little clothes. After his little sister, Gretchan, was born, my sewing knew no bounds. Alan's clothes had to be tailored in order to keep a masculine look, but with Gretchan, I could let my creativity soar. I haunted the remnant boxes in every shop that carried yardage, since it took very little material to make those garments. As Gretchan grew, I got plenty of practice, for she was always pleased with the clothes I sewed. I made her prom dress and, many years later, her wedding dress.

Alan and Gretchan, 1945. *Alan was a loving big brother to his newborn baby sister.*

CHAPTER THREE

1946 — 1976
MUSIC & MOURNING

Those of us who lived through the Great Depression and World War II truly appreciated the peace and prosperity which followed. For more than twenty years after the war ended, my life was filled with the sweetest melodies of life — a happy marriage to a fine man who loved his family and provided well for us, two beautiful children, a cozy home in charming Glen Ellen, California, caring friends, good health, much joy and laughter, and many more blessings. The harmonies and grace notes of those years will forever echo in my heart and memory.

Glen Ellen, California. *We moved to this friendly little town in 1946, thinking our stay would be temporary, but we remained here for more than thirty years.*

The Day My Hair Turned Grey

I am certain statistics would prove me wrong in my statement regarding my title to this story. In reality, the process of a person's hair turning grey is a gradual one, occurring over a period of perhaps many years. However, the following incident was so frightening that I tremble at the memory ... and I'm sure I aged at least a decade because of the experience.

My family and I were newcomers to Glen Ellen, having moved into the big old Chauvet house in 1946. This house was constructed by Henry Chauvet, along with a hotel and several other buildings in Glen Ellen's early days. Mr. Chauvet was one of the early settlers of the town and quite wealthy. He also owned a brickyard, one of two in the area. Several buildings made from the bricks from his brickyard still remain and are occupied. The house we lived in was occupied by the daughter-in-law of Henry Chauvet. A widow in her eighties, she had no need for such a large house, so she had converted most of the upper story into a rental apartment, and we were the lucky ones chosen to rent it at that time. The rooms were spacious with high ceilings and ornately formed moldings decorating the joining of wall and

Younkin Family in Los Angeles, 1948. From left to right, front row, Chester and Donald, Clarence's son; back row, Paul, Edna, John, Harold, and Clarence.

ceiling. Our apartment consisted of six large rooms divided by a spacious hall. One bedroom had a fireplace with a beautiful mantle. Approximately halfway down the length of the hall was an open stairway with nineteen steps leading to the first floor below.

At the top of the stairs was a gate which was kept latched. The reason for the closure was due to the fact that my daughter, Gretchan, was little more than a toddler at the time. Also, I was babysitting a friend's year-old boy, who was a whiz in his walker and never stayed in one place longer than a minute.

Gretchan and Alan, 1949. *In Glen Ellen, we lived in the historic Chauvet House, visible behind the children.*

One warm afternoon after both youngsters had finished napping, they were amusing themselves about the apartment when suddenly I heard a scream and a thud in the hall. I dropped whatever it was I was doing and made a mad dash into the hall just as that walker with the baby in it went bouncing down the flight of steps. And I was trying all the while to catch or delay his fall, but in the few seconds that transpired, I was unable to do so, even though we practically met at the foot of the stairs. Miraculously, the baby was still in his walker. Never in my entire life have I been so frightened. Terrifying visions of a mortally injured child raced through my mind, the innocent child of a friend who trusted me, a child who was my responsibility. I removed him from the walker, cradled him in my arms as he cried, and went back upstairs, still not sure of his condition. In a very short time he stopped crying and wanted to play. The only sign of an injury was a small bump on his head. He was also checked by a doctor that day, and he, too, found him in sound condition except for the small bump on his head. Surely we had an angel watching over us that day. But my hair never looked the same again.

Leave the Bees Be

During the fall of 1946 a painful and frightening event occurred during our family's earliest days in Glen Ellen. School was about to start, and Alan, who was six years old, was ready and eager to begin first grade. I went with him on opening day, which was a get-acquainted event with refreshments, and it was here that I became acquainted with another mother or two.

Our family was living in the old Chauvet house, one of Glen Ellen's first and finest homes, built in the early 1800s. It had long been lovingly cared for, but having stood for more than a century, it was beginning to deteriorate in various areas. One of these areas happened to be one or two small holes in the exterior siding adjacent to our living room. I wondered if this hole, or holes, could have been the handiwork of an aggressive redheaded woodpecker that dwelt in the area. I knew that there was at least one, for day after day I heard what sounded to me like a jackhammer drilling away on the side of the house.

He may have been drilling in search of insects behind that siding. And there were insects! Much to our distress, one would occasionally find its way into our living quarters and terrify us. We called them bees, but in reality they were not honey bees, but yellow jackets. They were definitely not friendly, but vile, vicious little insects. Gretchan was a mere two years of age and had already been stung by one of these nasty creatures, which was very traumatic for her ... and for her

Easter, 1949. *Above, Gretchan and Alan pose for a picture before church. Gretchen is wearing the new Easter outfit I made for her.*

mother. The situation was unbearable.

After several painful episodes when our landlady couldn't, or wouldn't, do anything to resolve the problem, that is, have the holes in the side of her house repaired, Byron decided to eradicate the pests once and for all. After first consulting our landlady about a method to remedy the situation, they agreed upon a plan to first eliminate the yellow jackets by spraying a powdered cyanide into the holes in the siding, after which she promised to call a carpenter to close the holes. Byron decided the spraying would best be done late at night when the pests would be dormant. At least, that was the assumption.

None too soon, the night came for action. Byron donned a face mask and gloves and, armed with a hand bellows and a supply of cyanide, climbed a ladder to the second story of the house where the problem existed and began to pump the poison into the hole with the bellows. Well, someone had by far overestimated the time of inactivity for those little pests. After the first two puffs of poison, their leader retaliated by summoning the entire population into action. They came out of the hole and attacked their aggressor with a vengeance. They were mad! Before Byron could make his way down the ladder, he had yellow jackets all over him in places he never dreamed they could reach.

The time was getting late, after nine o'clock. What a dilemma! Byron was starting to have difficulty breathing, with pain and swelling throughout his face. We were at a loss, we had only met one or two persons in this new community, did not know any doctors, nor where or if a hospital was anywhere nearby. The one person I felt closer to worked at a bar near Glen Ellen. Rather than trying to reach her by telephone, I hopped into my car and drove to the bar to seek her help. She immediately called her doctor and after explaining the situation to him, he told her to bring the patient to his office in Sonoma, a distance of seven miles, and he would meet us there. Byron's condition seemed to be worsening by the minute, so the friend and I lost no time getting him to the doctor's office. There, the doctor immediately began emergency measures, and within a very short time Byron showed improvement, breathing without difficulty. Then, suddenly, he became nauseated and, without warning, upchucked all over the poor doctor.

What an introduction to a doctor. Luckily for us, he held no grudge nor ill feeling. He became our family doctor for the next several years, until he became a surgeon. Possibly, he wished to avoid future confrontations such as we had put him through.

Cub Scout Pack Night — The Good, the Bad, and the Ugly

The time was near Halloween, and I believe the year was 1948 or 1949. Dunbar School in Glen Ellen sponsored, among other things, a pack of Cub Scouts, boys eight to ten years of age. Our pack consisted of several dens, and each den was made up of six or seven boys. Each den had a den mother assisted by a Boy Scout. They met every week, usually at the den mother's house, for their various projects and activities.

I was a full-time homemaker at that time, and when both my children were in elementary school, I volunteered for many positions when help was needed. In fact, I found it to be very rewarding and grew closer to them as we participated together in their activities. My stint as den mother also let me keep an eye on Alan and curb his antics a bit.

Once a month the pack met, each den demonstrating what they had accomplished in their weekly meetings. These were great times, when parents, siblings and friends enjoyed good fellowship and witnessed the accomplishments of their young budding artists, actors, writers, and creative geniuses.

My den, Den Number Two, decided to do a skit. Each boy already had his Halloween costume, so they brought those, and together we made up a skit. Buddy Adkins had all the trappings of a cowhand, so he was the Lone Ranger, Malcolm Weston came with a Bugs Bunny mask and some sort of suit, Jimmy Norrbom, the smallest boy in the den, dressed in a Pinnochio costume, another lad was outfitted as a scarecrow, and last, but certainly not least, was my son, Alan, in, of all things, a Satan mask and red "long johns" he had borrowed from someone. The last two boys in the den were equipped with sheets, so they became ghosts — after all, it was Halloween.

Then they all began to make suggestions — what each one would do and say. Their enthusiasm knew no bounds. The drama grew to magnificent proportions, so I had to remind them that we would have a limited time because the other dens would also have presentations to contribute.

The boys decided that I was not to escape participation in this production, so with a little compromise, they agreed to pantomime the action if I would read it. I may have changed the wording a bit and yes, condensed it, but in reality, the content of the whole skit must be attributed to six young, enthusiastic Cub Scouts, my son, Alan, among the six.

On the following page is the poem I wrote and read as my Cub Scouts pantomimed the action. It was a most ambitious production by six Cub Scouts. My only concern in the conclusion of this drama was the seemingly overly exuberant punishment they all joined in and inflicted on old Satan, portrayed by my son. But, perhaps they knew something I didn't.

One dark and stormy night
So I've been told . . .
Old Satan sat
A miserable sight to behold . . .

He sat there reading
The paper he'd brought
And as he read
His temper did grow hot.

For there before him
In big bold print
He read of the many
Good deeds and much content.

Ah yes — much to
His sorrow and dismay
Little Pinnochio has brightened
An old man's day.

The Lone Ranger, too,
To the rescue has come,
He saved a man's life
And maybe then some.

Bugs Bunny makes
Children happy as can be
CURSES! Such good
I simply cannot see . . .

Next came the scarecrow
All tattered and torn,
He frightened the last crow
From that field of corn.

Now Satan scowled
And Satan schemed
His evil plan
He soon dreamed . . .

A party!
A surprise t'will be
Then I'll fix 'em . . .
Just wait and see.

These good deeds have
Gone on long enough . . .
'Tis time I put an end
To all that stuff.

Came the hour of
Their arrival . . .
HORRORS! What chance
Their survival . . .

In came Bugs Bunny
His carrot in hand,
Then the scare crow,
Finest in the land.

Next little Pinnochio
With nothing to hide
And the Lone Ranger
Without his horse to ride.

Now here they were,
Suspecting not at all
That Satan planned for each
A horrible downfall.

Little did he know that
Ghosts prowled round about . . .
To his dismay he learned
Those ghosts did have clout . . .

They grabbed old Satan
Threw him to the floor,
Bound and gagged him,
And tossed him out the door!

Mid cheers and shouts of Joy!
I heard them all recite
HAPPY HALLOWE'EN!
And to all — Good night.

Marietta

The Duck Who Thought He Was a Dog

Around 1950, when Alan was about ten years old, someone gave him a little duckling. He was a most endearing little ball of yellow fluff, and the whole family, including our two dogs, Goldie and Inky, fell in love with him. With tender loving care, he thrived and in a short time grew into a handsome white duck who sported a topknot of feathers on his head. This little bunch of white feathers, rather than being centered on the very top of his head, was just a bit off to one side, giving him a kind of jaunty look to add to the character he was becoming.

The dogs accepted him as another member of the family, never barking nor in any way showing displeasure with his presence. Alan named him "Donald" and when called, he responded with an enthusiastic "quack, quack." No matter where Goldie and Inky went, Donald went along. Sometimes, when they got excited and ran after a squirrel or bird, he was hard pressed to keep up with them, since his short legs weren't half as long as theirs. But, he gleefully joined the chase, all the while echoing their excited barking. However, try as hard as he might, his bark always sounded like "quack." Goldie, who was a Cocker Spaniel, liked an occasional romp in the creek that ran behind our place, and, of course, this was a sport that Donald Duck excelled in with absolute ecstasy. It was amusing to watch the two of them cavorting and splashing in the stream, until the dog tired of it. Then she got out and shook the water off her coat, making a shower of drops, while the duck gave a fairly good imitation by shaking his feathers.

In the late afternoons, especially in the summertime, the dogs had a habit of watching for Byron's return home from work. Our house and yard were situated lower than the street level, so the dogs, accompanied by the duck, would make their way up the driveway to the street, and there settle down, a dog on either side of the duck, to watch and wait for the sound of his car. As the time neared for Byron's arrival, the duck always seemed to be the first to hear the car, and his head would rise up above the dogs, resembling a periscope. By the time the car came within a short distance of their watch-station, both dogs scrambled to their feet and raced down the hill, ready to greet their master when he stopped near the door of our house. This was their way of welcoming him home, and Donald, believing that he was a dog, was not to be outdone by either Goldie or Inky, even if he had to flap his wings extra hard to keep up with them.

Goldie had many lovable characteristics, among them her tolerance and affection for Donald. But there was one bad habit she had, which no one had been able to break. She loved to bark at the car's moving wheels, if no adult was in sight to restrain her. And, alas, this brings our story to a sad ending. One summer evening as Byron approached the driveway, the three sentries left their post, Inky took the usual path down into the yard, but Goldie decided to bark at the wheels of the car all the way down the driveway, with Donald close on her heels, rendering his version of barking. At the bottom of the hill the driveway made a curve into the yard. Goldie being nimble, leaped safely out of the way, but poor Donald, with his short legs and cumbersome body, fell beneath the wheel and there met his doom.

Ours was a house of gloom for days, and Alan mourned the loss of the duck to the extent that his dad felt it necessary to seriously explain to him that it had been an unavoidable accident. Also, he still had Goldie and Inky, both lovable pets, and there would be many more pets for him to love, and life goes on, the good along with the bad.

More Adventures with Family Pets

Our family members have always had an affinity for unusual pets. Or, perhaps it was the way they were treated or nurtured that made them seem unusual or unique in the things they did. There were numerous dogs, one being a lovable Cocker Spaniel, Goldie, whose tree climbing ability amazed everyone, especially the squirrels that scampered about the yard. However, after falling from the limb of a tree one day, she lost her enthusiasm for climbing, and thereafter, she ended the

My Precious Parents, 1951. *Mom and Dad, Edna Younkin, age 70, and John K. Younkin, age 79, posed with me while visiting my family in Glen Ellen. Mom and Dad enjoyed our pets, too.*

chase at the base of the tree, letting the squirrel, cat, or bird take refuge in the tree unscathed.

Then, of course, there was Alan's beloved Duck, who tried so hard to bark like his companions, the dogs Goldie and Inky, but could only elicit a weird imitation that was somewhere between a raspy yelp and a guttural growl. After he met his untimely and tragic demise beneath the wheels of a car, a friend, feeling empathy for Alan, came forth with what he thought would be a consolation and a replacement for the ill fated pet. His gift, not one, but *two* ducks, took up residence in our yard; rather, they spent most of their time hovered on the stoop near our front door, making that entry more than a little perilous for family and friends. The pair must have been twins, one as ugly as the other. They had not one redeeming feature that I could see. Each had what appeared to be an ugly red mask on his or her head, a characteristic of Muscovy fowl. And the word "foul" fit their dispositions. After enduring their very bad attitudes for a few days, we packed them into the truck one dark and cloudy night and delivered them to the park in Sonoma where there were two ponds and numerous ducks to keep them company.

Back at the ranch was another of our unique friends and family, a little parakeet the kids named Myrtle. We never succeeded in teaching her to talk, but she had a few traits of her own which she used to her own satisfaction. It didn't take her long to find that with a bit of pecking and maneuvering she could open the door of her cage and gain freedom. During one of these freedom flights, she discovered a taste for music. No matter how many times she was put back in her cage, sooner or later she opened the door, and then made her way to the piano where the rack was lined with sheet music. Myrtle didn't sing or play the keys, just nibbled every sheet of music. When the music was packed away out of her sight, she went for the venetian blinds. We finally resorted to wiring her cage door shut, making her a prisoner thereafter. It seemed such a shame, denying her freedom, but when she began her destructive nibbling on the lampshades we felt compelled to take more drastic measures.

Through the years numerous animals and birds were acquired and lovingly cared for. I could never refuse my youngsters' enjoyment of adopting as their own some special little creature; that is, until it came to a rat that Alan wanted to adopt in partnership with his best friend, Ryan. My tolerance for long-tailed animals had reached its limit. Alan's turn for housing the rat never came about.

That same year, for Easter, Gretchan acquired a tiny baby chick. I doubted that it would survive many days, but I must have underestimated the loving care Gretchan was to give this tiny yellow ball of fluff. Over the next few weeks it grew to be a beautiful little brown hen and was given the name of "Henrietta," later called "Henny Penny." She followed closely behind Gretchan whenever she was outside, all the while softly and contentedly singing her little chicken clucking sounds.

Henny Penny grew to maturity without knowing the companionship of like siblings. Gretchan was her family, and I guess it was her devotion to Gretchan that caused her to pay the only tribute she knew how to give. One day, while nestled at Gretchan's side, she stood and laid an egg at Gretchan's feet. We all marveled at such a feat.

The time came for the family's yearly vacation. We planned a rather extended time visiting faraway relatives in another state. This meant that some arrangement would have to be made for the care of little Henny Penny while we were traveling. One of Gretchan's friends volunteered to keep the hen, which seemed ideal because he lived on a small ranch where she would be housed with his family's chickens.

When we returned many days later, Gretchan was met with the shocking news that her loving little Henny Penny had met with a terrible fate and had become a meal for the family of her friend. We wondered but never learned if their chickens had possibly attacked and slaughtered the newcomer added to their flock. Gretchan found it very hard to forgive her friend's mother for having committed what she considered a most dastardly deed to an innocent creature. However, Gretchan was consoled by the fact that her little pet had not lived entirely in vain, but had served mankind in the way God intended.

Rain, Rain and More Rain

Unusually wet winters always bring to mind a similar rainy season in 1955 when I feared for loss of property and even life itself. I've always loved the rain, but sometimes one can get a little too much of a good thing. That year, the first storm blew in late in September, causing great consternation for grape growers, and continued through the rest of the year. I kept track of the days it rained: that fall we had one period of forty days of continuous moisture from above. Sometimes it was just a drizzle; other times, a real deluge.

We were living in a little cottage we rented on O'Donnell Lane in Glen Ellen. The stream that ran along the back of this property was Sonoma Creek, usually a picturesque little brook where my children and their friends spent many happy hours playing, catching tadpoles, frogs and, once in a while, a turtle. Several days of rain turned this quiet little stream into a raging torrent. Our house was probably about thirty yards from the edge of the creek and at least twenty or more feet above it, so we felt reasonably safe, even though the water had risen several feet and the current was swift as it rushed past, carrying trees and all kinds of debris. One morning it was most disheartening to see a frightened deer being swept along in that raging current. I never knew if it was rescued or perished.

On the opposite side of the creek from us the ground rose rapidly, covered with trees and other vegetation. This was the foot of Sonoma Mountain. Here, the real trouble began. One night, after many days of rain, a huge portion of this hill started sliding. Needless to say, it drastically changed the course of the creek. Our neighbor, whose property adjoined ours, and his neighbor were rapidly losing ground as the rushing water cut back into their properties. Their homes happened to be situated almost directly in line with the slide. From our window we watched our neighbor's guest house fall into the creek; his chicken house had disappeared during the night. By the time we witnessed two more buildings and a huge tree fall victim to the raging waters, we were starting to pack our most precious possessions in boxes and whatever our car would hold. Before leaving, however, the rain ceased, the sky cleared, the slide had more or less stabilized, and the water began to recede a bit, so we opted to wait and see, but the boxes remained packed and ready for a quick move. The hours grew into days, and with the welcome break in the weather, the water in the creek subsided to a more normal winter level and the imminent danger passed. Several families living on O'Donnell Lane, whose houses were closer to the creek than ours, suffered much damage from flooding. We considered ourselves very lucky, and remained in this house for two more years while we built our own house, which was also on O'Donnell Lane.

Love Thy Neighbor

Having grown up in a small town where you not only knew your next-door neighbor, but almost everyone in town; you knew their names and for the most part, something of their lives, good or bad. It was hard to imagine what life would be like in a big city where people had no contact with those living, traveling or working nearby. It must have been our good fortune to find, or to make friends among those people who were our neighbors or close associates through the years and in many different places. I have found that if you would have a friend you must first be one. My husband, Byron, was of the same mind.

One of the first projects Byron undertook in building our home in Glen Ellen was installing gates in the fences that separated our property from that of our neighbors. One was on the west, one to the north, and one to the east.

The south side faced the street and was open with a driveway. Byron and I had conferred with the property owners previously and they all thought the gates were a most friendly gesture. Our neighbors to the west lived in San Francisco and only came to Glen Ellen on weekends to work on their house there, preparatory to making it their permanent home. The same was true of the other two neighbors. Those on the east side of us, the Uptons, whose interim residence was a tiny trailer house, were elderly. "Old Joe" was in his eighties, a Jack of all trades who preferred the country life. His wife, however, who was about the same age, had an interest in a large nursery in the San Francisco area, and she preferred to commute each weekend to Glen Ellen. Each Monday morning as Joe put her on the bus, he'd wave good-by with this jaunty little departing message: "Bye Darlin'. Write if you find work." His sense of humor was always alive and well.

Joe was a character who kept us entertained with his many stories. He considered Byron and me his kids (he had none of his own) and our kids, mere babies, even though they were half grown. So the gate between us was a natural. Joe was constantly building, first a roof over the tiny trailer house, then a room to be used as a kitchen, then a cement patio, then another room, and on and on. I think the last thing he built was a carport. That just about filled the small lot. But still, he managed to have a little garden. He followed the current *Farmers' Almanac* closely and kept us informed of the proper times for planting and harvesting. We also had a garden and found his suggestions and advice most helpful. We didn't always plant the same things Joe did, so we had the added pleasure of exchanging our vegetables and plants with him. Among other things, he loved to fish, and he always shared his catch with us. He kept our freezer well stocked with fish.

It took two years of building to finish our house, and Joe was always available and willing to help in any way he could. When it came time to do the roof, Joe insisted on putting on the roofing material for us. Byron did not want this, since he knew Joe's many projects weren't built according to approved building codes. But Byron couldn't find a way to deny Joe this privilege without hurting his feelings, wounding his pride, and perhaps ending their friendship. So, Joe put on our roof. It wasn't executed exactly according to Byron's specifications, but it passed the final inspection in the end. So we lived with it. At last, the house was finished.

Dear old Joe spent countless hours seated at our kitchen table over a cup of coffee, spinning his many stories of past experiences of a most interesting life. These were interspersed with humorous quips and jokes and, frequently, a spell of coughing and gasping; he was quite a heavy smoker, rolling his own cigarettes, and suffered from emphysema. He had not married until he was past the age of sixty five. When a fishing buddy asked why he wanted to get married, Joe's reply was, "Want to? I had to."

He and Byron shared a love of electronics, radio and all things in that area. Joe had lots of music, made lots of recordings, and had speakers in many places in his house and yard. He had so much fun, mostly at our expense. When we had guests, especially in the summer when we'd be enjoying the yard or patio, there would come the cries of a baby being neglected, somewhere in the neighborhood. It was worrisome to our guests, but we knew it was just Joe playing tricks with his recordings. Another time it was the sound of a train, quite close, astounding a guest who wasn't aware that Glen Ellen had a railroad. It didn't, but it had in the early days, and with a little help from Joe's sound effects, it sounded like that old train was running again.

Alas, there came a day many years later when Byron found the gate to Joe's property closed tight and nailed shut. I never knew what happened, and if Byron knew, he didn't tell me. In truth, he seemed to be as puzzled as I was. Some words or some incident must have transpired. I could only hope that it might have been the foibles of old age — Joe was nearing 95 at that time. No more stories, no visits at the kitchen table, nothing but a void in our hearts.

This brings to mind a saying I have heard many times, "Life is fragile. Handle with care." And a favorite song keeps repeatedly playing in my head, the words of which are, "If I have wounded any soul today, if I have caused one foot to go astray, if I have walked in my own willful way .... Dear Lord, forgive."

Cherry Pickin' Time

In the good ol' summertime ... the livin' is easy ... no school lunches to pack, no school home work, few schedules to meet ... how sweet it is!

One warm sunny day many summers ago during the 1950s, a good friend told me of a certain rancher who had a large orchard with an abundance of cherries, more than he could use, and he was offering them to anyone who wanted to come pick them. It sounded like a mighty fine offer to me, a good chance for an enjoyable and profitable outing for my kids and also for my parents, who were visiting us from Los Angeles at the time.

We gathered buckets and bags and headed for the prospective bounty. My friend had given directions to reach the ranch, which was in the vicinity of Kenwood, California. This area was not extensively developed with housing tracts then, and the landscape was dotted with fruit orchards, small ranches and dairies, with many winding roads leading to ranches and an occasional vineyard.

We followed the directions carefully. We made our first turn onto

Lawndale Road from Highway 12 near Santa Rosa, California, and the going was easy. Then we turned onto a different road, the name of which I have forgotten. After a mile or so on this road, we came to a certain crossroad, the landmark being a yellow house surrounded by trees and a large garden. There, we made a right turn and traveled for another half- or three-quarters of a mile, and on the right side of the road was our destination: an orchard with countless numbers of cherry trees, all loaded with luscious-looking cherries.

I parked the car on the side of the road next to the orchard and we all piled out with bags and buckets in hand, each one of us eager to gather as many cherries as possible. Just like being turned loose in a candy shop, we attacked those cherries with gusto, eating as many as we put in our buckets. Oh how sweet they were!

About that time a car pulled alongside and a man got out and walked over to where we were busily picking. He casually asked how it was going; we enthusiastically greeted him and told him it was going fine, the cherries were delicious and plentiful. After a few more bits of casual conversation he informed us that we were in his orchard. The one we were supposed to be in was across the road. We had made a wrong turn at the last crossroad.

What a predicament — caught red handed, stealing cherries. I think we would have paid the man any amount of money, or labor, or anything, just to

Happy Home Life, 1953. *I was contented being a homemaker and mother in the 1950s, and Byron, Alan and Gretchen loved having me home.*

get out of this situation, and given him all of the fruit we had ripped off. We all felt like criminals — Dad and Mom, my two children, and I. But the man was gracious. Realizing we had made a mistake, he told us to keep the cherries, and he refused to accept payment for them. He said he had plenty left and that we needn't worry about the mistake. In fact, I believe he was thoroughly amused by the whole embarrassing event. No wonder those cherries were so sweet. 'Tis said, "Stolen sweets are the sweetest."

Optimism or Naivete

A recently published article about a young family from San Francisco becoming stranded on a lonely, snow covered road in Northern California, was tragic indeed, noting that the father perished while seeking help. Such an event always elicits many comments and suggestions regarding what might have been done to prevent the tragedy. Some proposed solutions are sound; others, overly simplistic. Who can fully understand the circumstances that prompt a family to leave a well-traveled highway and take a little known road in winter weather?

Once, long ago on a family trip, we did almost exactly the same thing. But since it was summer rather than winter, our story ended differently. We — Byron and I, our daughter, Gretchan, and her girlfriend Bonnie Charles — were coming home from a vacation in Oregon. The weather was very hot, and our car had no air conditioner. We were on the inland highway, the most direct and quickest way home, because Byron was due back at his job in the next two or three days.

Silver Anniversary, 1963. *Byron and I celebrated our twenty-fifth wedding anniversary with a small family party.*

By mid-morning we were still in Oregon, the temperature was

unbearably high, the car's engine was showing signs of overheating, and we felt like we were on the verge of heat stroke. So, we decided to take the next road with a sign directing us to the ocean. We soon found ourselves on a narrow, winding, mountainous road with forest all around us. In some places the road was so narrow that meeting another vehicle would have required us to back up to a slightly wider place so the oncoming vehicle could pass us. At one point, the road dipped into a ravine where we had to ford a small creek. Fortunately, there was only a trickle of water running over a bed of rocks, so that was no big problem. What a ride this turned out to be! But we were sure of two things: first, we were

GROUSE MOUNTAIN CHAIR LIFT
VANCOUVER, CANADA

Sky High. *On a trip to Vancouver, Byron and I rode in a chair lift, a first for both of us.*

headed in a westerly direction — our compass said so; and second, sooner or later, we would come to the coastal highway. We hadn't seen a soul on this road in all the miles we'd traveled since leaving the highway, and we were feeling grateful that we hadn't met a car or truck.

Then, just as we were beginning to feel the cool coastal air and our optimism was growing, our car's engine decided to quit. No amount of coaxing did a thing to get it started. It was dead. What a predicament — no phone or radio and miles from civilization. Before panic set in, I remembered my conviction of faith, that God gives special protection to children, drunkards and foolish ones. Well, we had two children, Gretchan and Bonnie, even if they were pretty well grown up. Possibly, we had double protection in that we were foolish for leaving the highway for an unknown route.

We sat pondering our fate while the moments ticked by, and in a short time a miracle happened. Our guardian angel was a trucker whose destination was the same as ours. He was familiar with the country, being a woodsman in this very forest area, and told us this was an old logging road. He promised to send help for us when he reached the next town. In a short time a tow truck appeared, and we were rescued and on our way to the Ford garage in Bandon,

Oregon. By the time we reached the garage it was nearly 4:00 P.M. and all but one mechanic and the manager had left for the day. This being a Friday, they were not due to return until Monday morning. Another dilemma! Our car needed a new motor, and none was available in this garage or town.

Wonders never cease, and we soon discovered we were to experience yet another blessing. The manager of the garage, upon learning that Byron was trying to meet a work schedule, assured us that he would help. He arranged for his mechanic to drive to Coos Bay, a distance of 100 miles, to get a motor, and install it upon his return. In the meantime this same man, our second guardian angel, obtained a motel room for us, and loaned us a car to use for the several hours it would take to get our car in running condition.

By noon Saturday we were on our way home. Monday morning found us in our old routines, gratitude in our hearts for being alive and well, for the kindness shown us by the thoughtful people who helped in many ways, and most of all, to God, who knows and controls all things.

A Musical Dream Becomes Reality

When I was a child and attended Great Bend's First Methodist Church with its large pipe organ, I dreamed of playing one of those grand instruments, but I thought that dream would never come true. Happily, although it would be many years later, my dream became reality.

Our little family moved to Glen Ellen, California in 1946, and within a short time began attending the little Glen Ellen Church on O'Donnell Lane. I started playing the piano for the children's Sunday School, and a short time later was asked to play the organ for church services. At that time the only

The Glen Ellen Church. *My family and I attended this church, where I played the piano and organ for services and events.*

instrument the church had was an ancient reed organ with pedals that took a lot of leg work to produce sound. It really wasn't much fun playing that old thing, but I felt that I was contributing a service to the church. Shortly thereafter, the members of the church began a series of fundraising projects and purchased a new electronic organ. I had the pleasure of playing that for the next several years. The little church was growing and prospering, and one day a large electronic organ was installed. What a thrill to play that instrument, for it had all the sounds of a pipe organ. This was the beginning of many interesting experiences for me.

With the growth of the church there was now the ability to include the organist in the budget, so I was now paid for doing a job I really loved. There were many weddings during the years that followed, which were always happy and exciting times for everyone involved, including me. No one could predict what might happen that was not scheduled during these ceremonies. One memory that occurs to me was the December wedding of a friend's daughter. The church was beautifully decorated with Christmas greenery for the evening ceremony, which would be illuminated by candlelight. The bride's attendants were clad in floor-length, red velvet gowns; the men, all in formal wear — white jackets with red cummerbunds and red bow ties. The bride's five-year-old sister and brother, twins, were ring bearer and flower girl, dressed exactly like the rest of the attendants. It was all so beautiful. As the twins came down the aisle to the first strains of the wedding march I noticed that the little boy had the biggest black eye, a real shiner. He had had an accident of some kind the day before the wedding. I thought of Norman Rockwell, and how he would have painted that scene.

At another time, I was playing for the wedding of a young man who had been in my Sunday School class several years earlier. This was a second marriage for both the bride and groom. His nine-year-old son and teenage daughter were their attendants. During the ceremony when the time came to produce the ring, the youngster reached into his pocket for it. Not finding it, his face revealed dismay, which quickly turned to panic as he searched for the missing ring, digging frantically into all of his pockets. Then, his father leaned over and began searching every pocket in lad's suit, causing quite an embarrassing pause in the ceremony. I saw a guest cover her face to hide a snicker and several others had sheepish smiles. Finally, at a signal from the minister, the ceremony was concluded without the ring. Later it was found in the church yard where the boy had stumbled and fallen before the ceremony. My sympathy was all for the boy, who was doing his best to fill the role of best man for his dad.

Then there was the wedding that was scheduled for 7:00 P.M. Usually I began playing about fifteen minutes before the ceremony was to begin, while the guests were gathering. A half hour passed, I had played all of the requested music, but received no clue to start the wedding march, so I went to other notes in my album, all appropriate for the occasion. Minutes ticked into hours, I had exhausted every piece of music in the book, and the guests were getting restless. Finally, when it was nearly 9 P.M., the wedding hostess came to me and said I might as well leave. The groom had missed his scheduled flight and wouldn't be arriving until later. Imagine the consternation that caused. I later heard they were finally married a little after 10 P.M., quietly, without music. But I got paid for my services, and got in an hour or so of extra practice.

The Church in the Wildwood

A long time ago, when I was a child attending Sunday School at the Methodist Church in Great Bend, Kansas, a favorite song of all the children was "The Church in the Wildwood." The words of the song, as well as the melody, were composed in 1857 by Dr. William S. Pitts after taking a stagecoach ride through the wooded valley of the Cedar River near Bradford, Iowa and envisioning a church there.

Several years ago while traveling through that part of our country, I had the opportunity to visit this little church. It has been preserved and maintained throughout many decades, becoming a national historical landmark. I was thrilled to realize that I was actually inside the little church we'd been singing about these many years.

In retrospect, I was struck by the similarity of this church to the one in Glen Ellen, which my family had attended regularly for many years. Except for the color of the paint (our church was white; the one in Iowa, brown) our Glen Ellen

Church in the Wildwood. *In the photo above, I am standing on the steps of the little Iowa church that was built after Dr. William Pitts envisioned a church in this bucolic setting in 1857 and penned his inspiring hymn "Church in the Wildwood."*

church closely resembled the one in Iowa in both original architectural design, Gothic-shaped windows, stately bell tower, and front entrance with several steps leading up to the doorway. Our family had attended services at the Glen Ellen church for as long as we lived there. Incidentally, the hymn 'The Church in the Wildwood" was often sung during Sunday School at our Glen Ellen church.

The Glen Ellen Church, originally established by the Congregational denomination, was built in 1894. Today, it is known as the Community Church of Glen Ellen, and as of this writing, it has a very active congregation. Services are held regularly and are well attended, as are the church's many related activities — Bible studies, prayer groups, and social events. Many weddings have been performed in the intimate, lovely chapel, heralded by ringing of the bell in the bell tower.

When I first attended the church, I wasn't favorably impressed. I thought the interior was unbelievably drab and dull. The walls were painted an ugly gray and seating was in straight-backed chairs similar to those in a dining room. I didn't realize at the time that the little congregation was struggling and couldn't afford better. But the people were friendly and welcoming, and before long I was bringing my children, Alan and Gretchan, to Sunday School there.

Even though only a small number regularly attended church services, there was always a church board, faithful and diligent in keeping the church alive and active in the community. The Sunday School thrived with the help of volunteers, mothers of the children mostly. The children were urged to invite their friends, which they did, and this helped to interest people in the church.

Through the years a succession of pastors served the Glen Ellen church, some for a short period of time; others, longer. Church membership and attendance gradually increased under the leadership of more than one dedicated pastor. The community in general began to be aware of this little church and become supportive of it.

Eventually, the congregation became more organized and plans were made to improve our church building. The men were the first to join together and form a work party. Remarkable progress soon followed. The interior of the entire church received new wallboard, new paint, and new carpet over the entire floor. Broken window panes were replaced with new colored glass, and candle brackets were installed on the walls. A congregation in San Rafael, which was in the process of remodeling and updating their church, gladly donated their old pews to us. Once the pews were covered with a

Younkin Siblings, 1969. *Above, I am surrounded by my brothers, from left to right, Chet, Paul, Clarence, and Harold. This photo was taken at our mother's funeral, the last time we were all together.*

coat of paint to match the interior of our church, our sanctuary was beautiful. Then, the father of three children in the Sunday School built a lovely altar.

Next, the women formed a club which we called "Mothers Club." We did not want to be known as a "Ladies Aid Society." That was from another era. The church still lacked many things, so Mothers Club began working to raise funds. Our first goal was the purchase of an electronic organ. The old-fashioned reed organ wheezed and rattled, and it was quite a spectacle when my tall friend Jane Bowman bumped her knees on the underside of the organ frame as she pumped those squeaky pedals. This was the first of many fundraising events, and as the town of Glen Ellen grew, so did the attendance of this, the only house of worship in Glen Ellen.

Among the earliest of our fundraisers was a variety show. We invited all organized groups, both church and community, to participate and the response was positive. Talent from our congregation included the church board,

Mothers' Club, and Sunday School classes. Joining us from the community were the Glen Ellen Fire Department, the Gemeni's Accordion Band, and a local dance class. The production was scheduled for two nights in Mayflower Hall, and played to a packed house both nights. On the first night of the program I became aware that we had a comic actor in our family.

Son Alan's junior high Sunday School class opted to pantomime a musical number that included two songs — "It's in the Book," and "Grandma's Lye Soap." Alan played the role of an old-fashioned, fire-and-brimstone preacher, and the rest of his class acted as his congregation. There stood my son before the podium, holding a Bible in one hand while gesturing with both hands, arms, and head as he "preached." Much to my surprise, Alan brought down the house with his performance. Wow! I didn't know my son was so talented. The elderly minister who was serving the church at that time laughed so hard I feared he might fall out of his seat. Years later, I was not the least bit surprised when Alan was given the leading role in his senior class play, *You Can't Take It with You.*

This was the first of many fundraising events that helped the Glen Ellen community become aware of our little church. In the years that followed, using the money we had raised, plus other contributions, more improvements to the building were steadily made, and the membership continued to increase until a full-time minister could be hired. Then things really began to move forward. Programs were instituted for young and old, and the spiritual life of the church and the community grew. God has truly blessed the diligent workers through the years as they labored to make this the lovely house of worship it is, the Community Church of Glen Ellen.

For more than thirty years I had the pleasure of serving as organist, and my children also had as their heritage the spirit of worship there.

Younkin Family Farewells

I loved my parents very much, and I was deeply grieved when they left this earth, even though I had faith that they were in a better place. Dad was the first to leave us, on March 1, 1953. Mother remained in their Southern California apartment until she, too, passed away, on September 18, 1969. My four brothers and I attended her funeral, and it left me with a bittersweet memory, for it was the last time we were all together.

More sadness came when I lost three of my brothers. Clarence, the eldest, died August 30, 1975; Chester, on May 14, 1991; and Harold, on September 26, 2004. Now, only Paul and I remain. Unfortunately, we do not live close to one another and communication is rare.

A Chinese New Year

The City of San Francisco, referred to as "the City" in surrounding cities and towns, has always held the utmost fascination for me with its many cultural facets, although I never desired to live there. The rural area of Sonoma County suited my life style most satisfactorily. Even my son, Alan, when quite young, used to say, "The City is a lot of fun, but I wouldn't want to live there." That was before he became an adult and went to work for the telephone company. He then spent several years living in the City, before he could move back to the country with his family.

A Very Good Year. *Byron and I were enjoying life to the fullest and dreaming about our retirement when this photo was taken in December of 1975.*

Although we visited San Francisco frequently during the years when Alan and Gretchan were growing up, it wasn't until sometime in the 1960s that their dad and I decided to attend Chinese New Year festivities, which took place late in January or early in February that year. We left home early in the day and upon reaching the city, left our car in a garage near Chinatown and went walking. It was fun window shopping and having something to eat in one of the many restaurants in Chinatown. It began raining, at times quite heavily, so we were in and out of the shops, enjoying everything while trying to stay dry.

As the time grew near for the parade, which was the main attraction we had come to see, we found a spot in the doorway of a shop along the parade's route. We were protected from the rain, but soon were joined by many others seeking shelter too. I began to wonder if I would be able to see anything since everyone was taller than I. During the time we waited for the parade to start, a woman with a big dog exited the door behind us and went somewhere, only to return a few moments later and disappear in the building. This occurred at least three times while we waited, and more people gathered in this spot. It seemed a bit mysterious, as she came and went without a word to anyone.

Suddenly, Byron, took my hand and told me to follow him. The mystery woman had quietly invited us inside to a better viewing spot. We followed her up an ancient stairway to a dimly lit hall. As we followed the woman down the hall, we were being observed. I noticed a couple of doors cracked sufficiently to allow pairs of eyes a peek at us. Then the woman opened a door to a room with a window overlooking the street. It was bleak and obviously unoccupied, with only a bare bed and a small lavatory in one corner. It was very eerie to me, and I could not help feeling uneasy when we were left alone. But the window did provide a perfect view. In a very short time the door opened and another couple was shown in. Still later, a man and wife and two small children joined us. Then the mystery woman returned carrying a basket laden with refreshments. She spread a clean cover over the bed and laid out an abundant array of snacks which she told us to enjoy while we watched the parade.

We were told by one person in the room that it is a Chinese New Year's Eve custom to invite whoever is on one's doorstep into their abode for refreshment. We learned that this building housed several old Chinese men in the rooms above the shop, and they had each contributed something toward

Apple Head Pioneer Dolls. *I made many apple head dolls during the 1970s, and my pioneer dolls, shown above, patriotic tableus, and others won blue ribbons at our county fair in 1975 and 1976.*

the snacks we had enjoyed while we watched the colorful dragons, elaborately decorated floats, and bands marching past in the rain.

Apple Head Creations

During the 1970s, the antique art of carving apple head dolls was revived, and articles appeared in magazines promoting the craft. It originally came into being at a time when the west was being settled. Pioneers were moving to a new land with their families, money was scarce, possessions were few, and toys for their children were mostly nonexistent. Sometime during this era, an enterprising person came up with an idea for carving an apple into the likeness of a doll. Thus, the apple head doll was created.

This craft became quite popular in recent years, with many articles appearing in numerous magazines describing the process of creating interesting apple head doll characters. I am uncertain as to how this was accomplished in pioneer days, but I proceeded to follow the instructions given in the present day method.

With but little carving experience, I chose a nice big apple, carefully peeled it, and started carving, first a nose, then eyes. Soon, it began to take the shape of a face. How exciting! I was on my way! A few more cuts and some shaving, and I had quite a respectable head with a complexion that was almost white, the color of freshly peeled apple. I was pleased with the results so far. The features in the carved face were of a young person or child. Now we come to the interesting part. The apple head must be dried in order to preserve it. This takes several days.

The apple is placed in a drying compound and completely covered with this material. While waiting for this process to be completed and to resist the temptation to peek at the head, I decided to work on the doll's body. I formed the armature, arms, legs and torso of heavy wire. The shape, or contours of the body, I padded with bits of cotton and remnants of material I had left from years of sewing. This step, forming the body, more or less depends upon the development of the head and what it looks like after the drying process.

After patiently waiting many days, I was finally able to unearth the head. The drying process had changed my carefully carved, youthful face into that of a much older character. This sparked my imagination. I would create an elderly figure, and I pictured a little grandmother. So I dug into my basket of knitting for gray yarn for my doll's hair. A flannel nightgown and yarn house slippers completed her costume. She was ready to be bent into whatever position I decided to pose her.

This, my first experience in creating an object that resembled a human figure, so pleased and excited me, that I could hardly wait to try my hand at another. Soon I had many apple heads in different stages of development. It was such fun to see how they changed in the drying process, my imagination knew no bounds. When the little grandmother figure turned out well, I thought she needed a mate, so I made a grandfather, bald with a fringe of hair. The first one, "Grandma," had tiny white beads set in her smile. "Grandpa" was toothless. Creating the clothing was no problem for any character I chose to make. Having sewn for myself and my two offspring, I had remnants of all kinds of fabrics.

So, many happy hours were spent creating the little characters that now occupy a glass-front case: little ladies dressed in their finest dresses with bonnets on their heads and toting baskets for shopping; two old gentlemen concentrating on a game of checkers (I also made their chairs, table and the checkerboard and checkers); Santa Claus, Uncle Sam, a couple (man and woman) in square-dancing pose, and many more.

In 1976, the year of the United States Bicentennial, the Sonoma County Fair Board chose as its theme "1776 — East and West." Inspired by Archibald M. Willard's famous painting, "Spirit of '76," I decided to enter a patriotic apple head doll tableau in the Arts and Crafts competition. I created a group of four figures, each clothed in a costume appropriate to that period of America's history. As I worked on the figures, I mentally kept time to the beat of the drums and the shrill notes of the fife that filled the air with a lively march tune. One figure proudly bore the flag with its thirteen stars as the group marched in cadence to the music, each figure raising a right foot in mid air, all in step to the march tune (as modeled in clay).

My only problem occurred with the drummer boy in the group. In the creation of an apple head character, much of his or her personality evolves during the drying process. As the apple shrinks over days of drying, numerous creases form, which take on the appearance of wrinkles, thus making it into an elderly character. Therefore, creating a youthful-looking drummer boy was somewhat problematic. Nevertheless, when I had finished, I had four apple head characters that reasonably resembled the "Spirit of '76" picture.

I happened to have an empty fish aquarium, which I lined with red, white, and blue bunting, and in this I placed the four little figures in proper marching position. On opening day of the fair my family and I were thrilled to find my project prominently displayed and brandishing a big blue ribbon, indicating first place winner!

The ensuing years brought many changes to everyone and everything.

Marietta's Paintings. *I have always enjoyed arts and crafts, and I've spent countless hours applying paint to canvas, ceramic figures, decorative plates, and many other items. My faithful german shepherd, Anka, whose portrait appears above left, and my dachshund/cocker spaniel cross, Inky, were faithful companions.*

Apple head art faded into obscurity along with other arts and crafts fads. My bevy of little figures, too, was undergoing change. Each year the heads continued shrinking, adding more lines and wrinkles in the faces as the color gradually darkened and changed from Caucasian to Hispanic to something darker, perhaps Indian, and finally, to African-American. I now had a black Santa, and numerous other little characters all an intense shade of black. Even my "Uncle Sam," dressed in red and white pants, blue star-studded vest, blue cutaway coat and red and white top hat, turned black. Now, there's nothing wrong with black figures, but that wasn't what I intended to create, so I discarded the overly withered noggins and replaced them with new heads, which I fashioned from clay, with features and color more in line with what I had planned in the beginning.

One of my favorite creations, a little grandmotherly figure, underwent the same type of surgery: removing the withered apple head and replacing it with one made of clay. Seated in a small rocking chair with knitting in her hands and her cat at her feet, she was ready for display at the following year's county fair. And this, too, won a first-place blue ribbon!

From Celebration to Mourning

Months before the exciting main event, excitement was growing in anticipation of celebrating our country's bicentennial — 200 years. Life was good, and everyone anticipated that 1976 would be a yearlong celebration filled with patriotic joy, fireworks, stars and stripes, and more.

The official bicentennial events began on April 1, 1975 when the American Freedom Train left Wilmington, Delaware on its twenty-one month, 25,388-mile tour of the forty-eight contiguous states.

On April 18, 1975, President Gerald Ford lit a third lantern at the historic Old North Church in Boston, symbolizing America's third century. The next day he delivered a speech commemorating the two-hundredth anniversary of the Battles of Lexington and Concord in Massachusetts, which began the military aspect of the American Revolution against British colonial rule.

There were many bicentennial festivities, including parades, concerts, and elaborate fireworks displays in the skies above America cities. Local observances also included painting mailboxes and fire hydrants red, white, and blue and, of course, flying American flags.

Queen Elizabeth II of the United Kingdom and her husband, Prince Philip, made a special state visit to the United States to tour our country and attend bicentennial festivities with President and Mrs. Ford. NASA commemorated the bicentennial by staging a science and technology exhibit housed in a series of geodesic domes in the parking lot of the Vehicle Assembly Building (VAB) called Third Century America.

Marketing of commercial products in bicentennial packaging was popular, usually distinguished by red, white, and blue patriotic designs. The official bicentennial star emblem was trademarked and only allowed to be used on products by paid license.

During this wave of patriotism and nostalgia that swept our nation, there was a general feeling that the angry era of the Vietnam War and the Watergate constitutional crisis of 1974 had finally come to an end. I remember early 1976 as a time of joyous anticipation of things to come. Work was plentiful, the economy was strong and, in general, life was most satisfactory.

In our own little corner of the world, Byron and I looked forward to sharing in some of the festivities, and we were dreaming about our future. It wouldn't be long until Byron retired from his job, after which he would enjoy leisurely hours woodworking in his shop. Together, we would work in the garden, pursue hobbies, and spend more time with our family. We planned to travel in our camper, visiting our daughter, Gretchan, and her husband, Joe, in Illinois, as well as relatives in other states.

Then, my world turned black, as black as the cancer found in Byron's lung on a routine doctor's visit in May. From this point on, it was a discouraging journey downward into the deepest, darkest canyon of despair, from surgery which was fruitless, through various forms of unsuccessful treatments, until November 5, 1976 when my beloved's life ended in a very painful death. We had been married thirty eight years, and what was "supposed" to have been would never be. But what was to be would change my life forever.

"There is in every true woman's heart
a spark of heavenly fire, which lies dormant in
the broad daylight of prosperity;
but which kindles up, and beams and blazes
in the dark hour of adversity."

Washington Irving

Brotherly Love, November 1976. *After losing Byron, I very much appreciated the love and support I received from my brothers, left to right, Harold and Paul.*

CHAPTER FOUR

November 1976 — 2006
MIRACLES & MARRIAGE

W hen an unexpected and unusual blessing occurs during a difficult time in life, why do we call it a miracle when in reality it is simply an answer to prayer? After all, God is the creator of all things, including miracles.

With Byron's passing in November 1976, I realized that life as I had known it up until this time had come to an end. He had always been my mainstay, supportive in every way, providing for the needs of our family, and lovingly filling the role of head of the family. At first I thought I couldn't go on, but I knew I must.

The time had now come to take stock of my assets and liabilities and get on with my life. Thankfully, during Byron's and my marriage, he had always made me a truly equal partner and we had made all major financial decisions together. So, I was fully aware of our finances and responsibilities, and I was intellectually capable of managing them. Finding the money to cover necessary living expenses was another matter. Because my beloved had died before reaching retirement age, his insurance had covered little more than burial expenses, and although he had made the final payments on our home mortgage and car, our savings were meager, and I knew I would need to procure some form of employment if I wished to live independently, which was of the utmost importance to me. So I prayed, asking God to open a door somewhere with the opportunity to make it on my own.

Within days, perhaps a week, my telephone rang one morning, and the very pleasant voice of a woman I'd never heard before, a hospital supervisor, asked if I'd be interested in a part-time job in the Medical Records Department of Sonoma Valley Hospital. She suggested I think it over and call her if I was interested. Could this be the answer to my prayer? I felt sure it was. My spirit was uplifted, and I took heart knowing that with God's direction and help, I could make it on my own.

Still, this new opportunity had happened so quickly that I was somewhat overwhelmed, but I pushed aside the doubt, returned the supervisor's call, and she scheduled an interview for me on the following day. As the time approached for the appointment, I was assailed with many more doubts and fears, so it was with much apprehension that I entered the medical records room, a place I'd never visited before, to meet people who were total strangers.

My nature is one of shyness, with difficulty meeting and opening up to new people. The supervisor of this department was a very warm and pleasant young woman who immediately put me at ease. After a few questions she took me to one corner of the room where I was seated at an electric typewriter, which was completely foreign to me. She gave me paper, placed headphones on my head, put a tape in the Dictaphone and told me to proceed. Imagine my astonishment to hear the familiar voice of the doctor I had worked for a few years previous to this time, and from whom I had gained medical terminology experience. Even though I had not worked for several years, her voice, which had been extremely hard to get used to, was familiar to me. I remembered her format, so I forgot all apprehension and typed away until the supervisor tapped me on the shoulder and told me I'd passed the test. The job was mine.

I started the new job and within a very short time became a full-time medical transcriber (today these professionals are called medical transcriptionists, but in those days, we were transcribers), at the same time learning new phases of the job. I mastered a comprehensive study of medical terminology for pathology, which I found interesting, and was soon assigned all of the typing for a pathologist. In addition, I did the regular medical typing for approximately twenty doctors of varied specialties who served Sonoma Valley Hospital. There were four other full-time medical transcribers besides myself, and two relief transcribers. I found them all to be congenial and helpful, making for a pleasant work environment. Earning my own money gave me a sense of exhilarating freedom, as well as responsibility, keeping abreast of household expenses, car upkeep, taxes, etc. Happily, my work as a medical transcriber sustained me until retirement.

Mine was a daytime shift, so I was always able to arrive back home before darkness descended. Evenings and weekends were my loneliest and most difficult times without Byron. Yet, I wasn't truly alone. I had my beautiful and faithful dog, Anka, who was always waiting to welcome me home. She was a source of security for me, ever watchful and alert, ready to protect me. She was my furry protector and my dear companion. Then, most important of all, my children were only a phone call away — Alan, in Petaluma, and Gretchan, in Healdsburg. They and their children would help me if needed, and they lived only a few miles distant. I also had good neighbors.

Time and labor are great healers. Family and friends are also a help. During my time of healing, my blessings were many. I continued serving as organist in the little church I loved, which was only a short distance from my home, and joined in family gatherings and church events whenever they occurred. Looking back, I am glad that I decided not to dwell on my past pain and loss, but to step forward into the future.

A Week of Pure Luxury

During the late 1970s I was alone and had a good job, and when vacation time came, I took my granddaughter Heather Huffman, who was in high school at that time, to Hawaii. She appreciated the gift of time and travel so much that she promised that one day she would take me on a vacation.

Some twenty years later, Heather was married, had a family, and a job at which she earned a generous salary. She informed me that the time had arrived for her to keep the promise she made long ago, and she offered me three or four different possible vacation ventures. I chose a cruise to the Mexican Riviera. It would be a new experience for both of us.

Early on the first day of February we boarded an airplane in Oakland and flew to Los Angeles, where we were met by a shuttle, which transported us to the harbor. Awaiting us there was an enormous cruise ship, ready to receive its passengers. Once we were aboard, we found our cabin, where our luggage was waiting, and we settled in for the first bit of luxury. The cabin had a nice window, and was otherwise beautifully furnished with everything we might need.

Heather had maps, charts, and brochures of everything that would be happening in our week of luxurious living. Having been told about the delicious and ample quantities of food served on these cruises, we made our way to the dining room to a wonderful buffet. There were so many delicious salads and all kinds of food, it was hard to restrain ourselves, knowing this was only the start of the week. Seating in this area was filling up fast when two ladies asked if they might share a table with us. They appeared to be most congenial, and like us, ready for adventure, so we welcomed them heartily.

In the conversation that followed, we learned that they were cousins who had recently found one another by way of the Internet, and they were having a great time, One woman, Claudine, revealed that she was paying for her cousin Theresa's cruise. This was a bit of information we could have done without since we noted Theresa's embarrassment at the remark. It was evident that Claudine was the most affluent, judging by her expensive suit, the many diamond rings she sported, and her attitude of superiority. Secretly, Heather and I called her as Mrs. GotRocks.

At dinnertime Heather and I found our assigned table, and there met a friendly couple celebrating their fiftieth wedding anniversary. Heather is very adept at opening a conversation, so it wasn't long before we discovered that we had something in common with this elderly couple. They told of having an interest in an orphanage in Mexico, which their church helped sponsor and which they planned to visit. Imagine our surprise to learn that it was the orphanage where Heather's parents, my son, Alan, and daughter-in-law, Margie, spent many weeks every year, doing volunteer work. How amazing that of the two thousand people aboard this ship, we should meet someone who knew not only the location, but the names of some of the staff of the same orphanage we were familiar with. We enjoyed their company, as well as the gourmet dinner served so elegantly.

Following the wonderful dinner, Heather and I strolled around a bit, looking through some of the shops. Then we entered the theater, where the seats were the most comfortable we'd ever had the pleasure of sitting in. The show that night featured a juggler, whose act was superb. The talented fellow juggled a bowling ball and other challenging object, and received generous applause from the audience.

The next day Heather and I explored the different areas of the ship and the weather was perfect for strolling the deck. Word came from the ship's captain that this was the season for whales in this area, and we were advised to watch for them. We watched for quite a long time, but, unfortunately, we didn't see any whales.

That evening at dinner two very pleasant ladies were seated at our table, completing the number of persons assigned to each table. One lady, Betty Jean, and the other, Barbara Jane, became the "B.J.s," our private title for their identity.

After dinner and before time for that evening's theater performance, Heather suggested that we visit the casino. We had been warned by her dad to avoid this, but since he was not around to enforce his warning, we wanted to have a look. The bright lights, the jingle of coins dropping into trays, and the whirring of slot machines was all fascinating, but a small voice whispered in my ear, "Get out of here. You don't believe in this." But on the other shoulder a little demon kept pulling my ear, whispering "Oh come on, you're on vacation, You only live once, and you might hit a jackpot." He even caused me to trip, and when I regained my balance, there I was right in front of the cashier's counter. What else could I do but buy a roll of quarters and head for a machine.

Heather had already selected a machine and was happily playing. I passed by her, heading down the road of degradation, and began feeding my quarters into that wicked machine. When I was down to the last three quarters, there came spinning up three cherries in a row, and when I pushed a button, the quarters came raining down into the tray. I promptly gathered them all into my cup and headed back to the cashier and traded them for currency. It was twice the amount I had put in. Thus ended my gambling career.

By Tuesday morning the ship had reached the southernmost point of our excursion and docked at Cabo San Lucas. We joined others going ashore and boarded a bus for a tour of the city and shopping. The tour ended when we were driven to a vista point where the Sea of Cortez joins the Pacific Ocean, then our bus returned to the dock where we boarded the ship.

The ship was now moving northward, and the next day docked at Mazatlan. Again we went ashore, this time taking a taxi to the town's center, which of course was the shopping and restaurant area where all of the tourists gathered. Heather and I found a small restaurant and enjoyed a lunch of tacos and margaritas. That day happened to be my birthday, February fifth, and I was content with our quiet celebration. However, when we had almost finished our meal, out of nowhere, it seemed, a mariache group appeared, and I was serenaded with a lively rendition of "Happy Birthday" in Spanish. The singers added more verses, but since they sang in Spanish, I couldn't understand them. Nevertheless, the surprise serenade was colorful and fun, and I was also treated to a big, delicious piece of chocolate cake with a candle on it. Soon, it was time to return to the ship.

That evening was Italian night, so the waiters dressed in the colors of Italy's national flag, and our dinners were authentic Italian cuisine. When the dessert course was served, a whole string of waiters surrounded our table and placed a beautiful birthday cake in front of me. It was the most beautiful cake I had ever seen, with my name on it and candles too. Then I was serenaded by all the waiters and everyone at our table, plus guests at a couple of other tables nearby. What's more, earlier in the day I had found a huge bouquet of lovely roses in my room. Talk about luxury. I felt like I was a winner on "Queen for a Day."

We had one more port to visit. The ship docked the next morning in Puerto Vallarta. Our adventures that day included a precarious walk across a stream that divided the town of Puerto Vallarta. The bridge was a swinging foot bridge, old and rickety, and did it swing! With every struggling step either of us tried to negotiate, we giggled at how foolish we must look, but we finally made it to the other side of the stream, having provided a bit of entertainment for fellow tourists.

After a bit more time exploring shops and walking to the beach, it was time to make our way back and find a taxi to take us to the dock where the ship awaited us. With the sun sinking into the sea, we were treated to the most magnificent sunset imaginable.

In just a short time, this day would end with a spectacular food display. The midnight buffet was indescribable. The delectable elements of numerous menus were all artistically arranged as only an artist could envision. Even though I was not hungry, I could not resist sampling some of the wonderful culinary delights.

Only one more day and we'd return to earth and the daily routine of life. The last day of the cruise was spent leisurely wandering about the ship, mostly observing various games and contests.

Our week of luxury ended on Sunday morning. Heather's husband, Randy Barnes, met us at the airport, and we were soon at their house in Pacifica where a lovely surprise awaited Heather. While we were away, her parents, Alan and Margie Huffman, had completely redecorated her living room, kitchen and dining room in bright wallpaper and sparkling white paint. We also received an enthusiastic greeting from Heather and Randy's three youngsters, who had helped their grandparents. Brittany, the eldest, had a lunch prepared for us, while her brothers, Justin and Caleb, proudly displayed their week's school projects. It was a joyous homecoming!

New Romance with an Old Friend

"Like the poetic rhythm of his long ago poem,
we fell in step together for a time such as this."

Marietta Younkin Showalter

Kenneth Showalter was a first cousin to my husband, Byron, and during the late 1930s when Byron and I were newlyweds, we used go out with Kenneth and his wife, Glenna. They had a car and they liked us. They would pick us up some Sunday afternoons and we would all enjoy being together. A time or two we went on a picnic, but mostly, we would ride around in their car and simply enjoy visiting with one another. We were always friendly —

but they lived in the country and we lived in town. Now, although we were quite fond of them, we thought they were country bumpkins. They, on the other hand, probably believed that we town folk lived a life of undeserved ease and had it made. Possibly, they envied us because we lived in town. We envied them because they had a car. When their children came along, they had a built-in babysitter with a grandparent who lived with them. So, for what it was worth, we had greater reasons to envy their country living. Both couples were assuming certain aspects of the others' lives which were not necessarily accurate.

When Byron and I moved to Omaha, we sometimes returned to Great Bend to visit Kenneth and Glenna. Suffice to say, when the visits faded, we remained good friends from a distance throughout many decades.

Kenneth lost his longtime love of more than forty years, Glenna, in 1974. Two years later I lost Byron. What was yet to come would transform the past friendship of two couples into a merging of two people. I considered Kenneth a friend, visiting with him during a couple of family trips back to Kansas in our later years. Little did I realize that he would take a liking to me while he was on a trip to California.

I was naive. I didn't pick up on the fact that his visit may have had an undercurrent. He stayed in my home in the extra bedroom. I didn't think a thing of it, but I sure worried about how that might look to outsiders. The visit was a time of visiting. It was merely a friendly get-together where the past had been bridged into the present. Our spouses were no longer living, but we found an innocent connection of camaraderie in our losses.

Once he returned home to Kansas, letters from Kenneth began to trickle into my O'Donnell Lane mailbox. As the letters increased in number, Kenneth's intent began to take shape. While I did not think Kenneth more than a friend prior to this, these letters began to change me. I knew in my heart that he was lonely and that he was seeking companionship with me. I began to soften to the idea. Thinking things through, I realized that the two of us could form a tender bond. In truth, it had to be that kind of relationship, because I did not desire to allow anyone to take Byron's place.

One of Kenneth's most touching tokens of affection was a poem he wrote for me, expressing his loneliness and longing to be with me. That poem still hangs in my home on a lacquered plaque which expresses his dreams and hopes of one day holding my hand in his hand.

Now aware of Kenneth's deeper feelings for me, I told him that I didn't see any marriage to anyone in my future. My life had been good with Byron and no one could take his place. Thankfully, I had the counsel of two wise women in my life: Dorothy Spratt, a longtime friend from Glen Ellen; and Gretchan, my daughter. Both of them talked with me independently and shared their thoughts. Gretchan said, "Mom, I am worried about you out here alone. Kenneth is a good man and he is a Christian." Dorothy said something similar, but added something more. "Now, Byron had his place and Kenneth has his place. But they don't overlap." A different outlook evolved in my mind after this advice. I knew what they said was true, and I began to soften to the idea of accepting Kenneth into my future as more than just a cousin of Byron.

I accepted Kenneth's persistent affection and agreed to marry him in 1980. Within weeks of my accepting his marriage proposal he arrived in California with his pickup truck packed so full that when he came across the California state line, the inspector looked into the truck and said, "Oh my gosh, go on!" Kenneth got a big kick out of that and would later love telling that story to others.

Two days later, on September 6, 1980, we were wed in the little Glen

Marietta and Kenneth's Wedding Day, September 6, 1980. *Our wedding party consisted entirely of family members. From left to right, front row, bridesmaids Laura McBurney and Heather Huffman; matron of honor, my daughter, Gretchan Huffman McBurney; the bride and groom, Marietta and Kenneth Showalter; best man, Kenneth's son-in-law, Roland Reese; ushers, Kenneth's grandson, Daryl Reese and Marietta's grandson, Vernon Huffman; and Bryan McBurney, candle lighter. In the back, left to right, are Dorothy Spratt, Pastor Gordan Johnson, and Rosemary Thomas, the organist.*

Ellen church, which Kenneth happily joined. The plans for this special day had begun long before his truck arrived, however. We thought about the plans carefully and decided to weave our children and grandchildren into the fiber of the wedding day. My daughter, Gretchan McBurney, was the matron of honor, my young granddaughters, Heather Huffman and Laura McBurney, were bridesmaids and my son, Alan Huffman, gave me away in marriage. Kenneth's son-in-law, Roland Reese, was his best man and his grandson Daryl Reese, along with my grandsons, Vernon Huffman and Bryan McBurney, were ushers. Kenneth's granddaughters Donna Stejskal and Deana Reese also participated. That was the entire wedding party — our family. After the ceremony, we all celebrated together at Dorothy and Jack Spratt's home in Glen Ellen.

Our honeymoon consisted of a road trip through Oregon and Washington. We took the scenic route and circled back down to California. It was a trip of enjoying each other's company and feeling warmly assured that we would return home to settle in and begin a new chapter in our lives.

From that time on Kenneth began to improve our home. He loved the holidays and decorated everything. Lights hung from eaves and tinsel dangled from ceilings. He literally made our house a fairyland. Colored lights blinked from room to room and the outdoors glowed. He built a miniature village in the yard complete with a little church, a store, and a couple of little houses. Each building was lit from within. It was a village created in his spare time and it glowed like our house during the holidays. One year he created a stable scene with life-size replicas of Joseph and Mary. Kenneth's creativity was a complement to my own. What he could create, I could enhance. Often, what I created, he would enhance.

The day of September 6, 1980 Kenneth and I joined forces in marriage — a tender union — one that would result in over twenty years of loving companionship. It would be two decades of friendship that blended our talents, nurtured intricate works of art by each, involved travels from Alaska to Mexico and from the Pacific to the Atlantic. Kenneth never did take Byron's place as I had once feared. Rather he complemented my life with his own. Like the poetic rhythm of his long-ago poem, we fell in step together for a time such as this.

North to Alaska

On July 6, 1992, very early in the morning, with all systems ready to go, Kenneth and I asked God's blessing and protection. Then off we went to meet my son, Alan, and his wife, Margie, in Healdsburg, California and continued northward, stopping for lunch in the redwood forest. The drive up the Avenue of the Giants was always a blissful experience; the quiet majesty of those huge redwood trees filling the air with their fragrant freshness made us want to linger in that peaceful area, so we made our way slowly. Late afternoon found us settled in among hundreds of other campers along the beach in northern California, one of many free campsites.

In the morning we continued on into Oregon, whose coastline was picture-postcard perfect. A stop at the cheese factory in Bandon probably raised our cholesterol several points by the time we'd tasted all the free samples. Farther north, we left the coast and headed inland to Portland, following the Columbia River until we crossed into Washington where the wheat harvest was getting into full swing. Soon we were in the beautiful area of Coeur d'Alene, Idaho and headed for another free camp site, this time alongside Lake Kilarney. That night a full moon sent shimmering beams of light through the pine trees onto the lake. The sight was so incredibly lovely as the water glistened and sparkled in the moonlight, it inspired me to try to capture the scene on canvas. I don't think I could ever do justice to such beauty, but I do have the picture framed and hanging on my wall.

Crossing into British Columbia, we encountered our first glimpse of a moose in the wild. The countryside was lush and green, varying from mountainous to rolling hills to flat land. Extensive fields were covered with bright yellow, which we thought to be mustard but learned that it was canola, one of Canada's most profitable crops.

Since we had heard so much about the gigantic mall in the city of Edmonton, Alberta, we decided to satisfy our curiosity. It was well worth the extra miles and time to see this man-made wonder, which contained more than 800 shops, a numerous variety of restaurants, gift shops, theaters, a hotel, skating rink, water shows with porpoises, a submarine, a swimming pool which had waves like the ocean and huge water slides. Beside all this, there was a complete Fantasy Land with all kinds of rides, including a roller coaster; and all this was under one roof.

Another two days of travel, much of it in the rain, which we enjoyed, and we reached Dawson Creek, British Columbia, the official beginning of the Alaskan Highway. Here we spent time in the museum and watched a video showing the building of the highway. This 1500-mile highway was built in a little less than a year by the Army Engineers, furnishing an important supply line to the interior of Canada and Alaska during World War II. The fiftieth anniversary of its completion was celebrated in 1992, so there were many celebrations, souvenirs, etc. along the way to Fairbanks, Alaska. Most of the tales and warnings we'd heard about the highway being so rough and bad were unfounded. Some stretches of graveled road forced us to drive more slowly, but we didn't mind, for it gave us more time to enjoy the magnificent scenery. Fireweed all along the way covered open spaces and roadsides with a carpet of pink, and the wild clover, which grew so tall we could scarcely believe it was clover, also added beauty to the scenery.

A few miles beyond Watson Lake, British Columbia we encountered our first real road trial: a section of highway was being reconstructed. When Canada builds roads, the road bed is built of rock, possibly boulders. As we bounced over mud, rocks and boulders at a speed of ten to fifteen miles per hour in the rain, a couple on a motorcycle started to pass us, and when they hit an exceptionally deep rut, the cycle tipped over, spilling the lady passenger directly in front of our vehicle. That was when we knew for a certainty that we had good brakes.

Along the way we saw antelope, moose and mountain sheep. Several miles through incredibly beautiful country we reached the town of Whitehorse in the Yukon Territory. After getting settled in our camp, we got on our bicycles and toured the region, ending in the local city park where a celebration was in full swing observing the seventy-fifth anniversary of Canada's Parks and Recreation Department A gigantic birthday cake was being served to any and all who came to the park.

The premium attraction in Whitehorse is the SS Klondike National Historic Site. This 210-foot sternwheeler carried passengers and cargo between Whitehorse and Dawson City on the Yukon River from 1937 into the 1950s. We were given a tour of the ship, which we found very interesting.

In the evening we attended a stage play, "Frantic Follies." We were in for a surprise when Kenneth, much to his chagrin, was picked out of the audience to come on stage and be a part of the production. Secretly, I think he rather enjoyed the special bit of attention. After some little ballyhoo, he was presented with a certificate naming him "Official Garter-Watcher of the Yukon," this after he had removed the garter from the leg of one of the cancan dancers and received a big smack on his forehead from another dancer. He didn't wash his forehead for two days for fear he'd wash away that kiss. For years he kept the garter as well as the certificate in a frame.

On July 20th, 1992, almost two weeks from our starting date, we reached the Alaska state line. The mosquitoes were getting more numerous, bigger and meaner. Just 98 miles from Fairbanks we encountered the Trans-Alaskan Pipeline, which stretches 800 miles from Prudhoe Bay on Alaska's North Slope to Prince William Sound, Port of Valdez.

Another day's travel brought us to the town of North Pole, Alaska. We just had to take pictures here and purchased postcards which we took to the post office so that they would carry the "North Pole" postmark to the folks back home. Only a few more miles and we reached Fairbanks, our northernmost destination. We planned to visit Denali Park, but it would be days before we could get reservations. This is a million-acre preserve, the largest in the United States. Meanwhile, we toured the area in and around Fairbanks, home of the University of Alaska. On the campus was a history museum, and we spent several hours there viewing the many exhibits showing Alaska's history, resources, native heritage, and culture. We also enjoyed a special concert performed by a children's orchestra. The maximum age of the performers was ten, several were much younger. I was totally fascinated with those tiny violins, cellos and other instruments, and by the expertise with which those cute little musicians played not one, but several numbers.

As the day wore on, we left the museum and headed for Denali Park. We were amazed at the number of RVs parked in the Visitors Center. It was quite a wait, standing in line in order to pick up our reservation. Since it would be two more days before our tour of this attraction, we drove a short distance to a large graveled area along the Nenana River where there were a hundred more campers awaiting their time to tour the park. We all enjoyed this time by relaxing from our days of driving. Alan caught up on some of his reading, Margie and I both painted on our projects, while Kenneth cleaned a number of my paint tubes. A pleasant hike along the river rewarded us with a collection of unusual rocks, and there was even an hour here and there for a game we like to play, Triominoes.

At last the time had come when we were to board the tour bus that would take us through this vast expanse of wilderness. We had packed our lunches, for there were no fast-food restaurants in the park. Private cars were not allowed past the fourteen-mile point, and one could see why. The road became one lane and unpaved, climbing steep and winding trails and, at other times, dipping down into valleys and over rivers. We saw lots of wildlife in their native habitat; first a bunch of ptarmigans, later some foxes, many caribou, grizzly bears, moose and Dall sheep. Our tour ended eight hours later back at the park's visitors center, a busload of tired but happy tourists, who had witnessed some of nature's pristine beauty.

The day following our tour of Denali Park, we left camp on a bright, beautiful morning and within a few miles Mt. McKinley came into view. This was a real thrill, because this snow-covered mountain peak, the tallest on the North American Continent, is rarely visible, only a few times a year. It is generally shrouded in clouds, but this sunny morning it was picture perfect, so, of course, we stopped in more than one spot along the highway to photograph this phenomenon, as did many of the other travelers. No one wanted to miss this rare opportunity. In a very short time it was again hidden from our view. We continued on to Anchorage, our next stop, and found the huge shopping complex, Diamond Center, where we planned to spend the next two or three days. There must have been at least five hundred RVs of every make and description in the area adjoining the paved parking lot, all neatly lined up in rows, so we just added our two vehicles to this city of traveling homes on wheels.

The following paragraphs contain the names of persons and places which require a little background explanation. In 1940 my brother-in-law, Vernon Huffman, Byron's brother, took his family to Alaska and homesteaded a large acreage of land a few miles from Anchorage, which was a small city at that time. He cleared the land, built a home, and raised his family there. Byron had wanted to visit Vernon in this northland, but both Byron and Vernon passed away before that dream could be realized. Although I would have preferred visiting Vernon's community with Byron, it was emotionally satisfying to do so with Kenneth, Alan and Margie. They were, after all, part of Byron's and Vernon's family.

From our parking site in Diamond Center, we drove a short distance to Huffman Square — named for Vernon — where we shopped, visited a laundromat and had dinner, later discovering Huffman Road, which was by then a main artery into the city of Anchorage. There also was a modern elementary school bearing the name Huffman.

The next day we rode the city bus to downtown Anchorage where we spent several hours in the art gallery of the museum. The paintings were outstanding, both oils and watercolors, all Alaskan scenes. There were also collections of ivory carvings and exhibits of native costumes and artifacts.

We had lunch in a mall, another gigantic complex filled with shops of every kind. Beside every store, home, parkway and along the sidewalks there were flowers — hanging baskets filled with bright blossoms. Many of these had deep blue lobelia growing so profusely it gave the appearance of huge blue balls with varicolored flowers blooming out the top, the containers being completely covered.

Before leaving home, we were told by Vernon's son, Jack, to contact a personal friend of his dad, Jean Smith, when we reached Anchorage. She was the person who had handled all of their real estate transactions. She was very friendly and congenial, and eager to give us a tour of Vernon's original homestead.

It was hard to imagine how this land must have looked when Vernon and his family lived there in years gone by. Since then, it has been subdivided into one- and two-acre lots, with large, beautiful homes occupying each one.

The winding paved streets all carried names of Vernon's family: Huffman Circle, Jack, Nancy, Sue, Evelyn (Vernon's wife) and on down to his grandchildren's names. The original house he built still stands, although it has been remodeled. Within close proximity is a huge nursery and a large gift store. Alan was quite impressed to have seen the imprint that his uncle, an unassuming man from Kansas, had made on this bit of Alaska.

It was now a month since we had left home on our journey to Alaska. Each day brought new sights and experiences, and we never ceased to be amazed by the awesome beauty of America's last frontier. We had dined like kings on fresh salmon — absolutely no comparison to the frozen kind we get at home — also moose burgers at the home of Margie's cousin, whom we visited. Her home was situated on the shore of a lake named Big Lake, near the town of Wasilla. Her husband had been on a moose hunt a few days before and had been successful, so their freezer was well stocked . We found it to be quite tasty.

I was never able to get used to going to bed when there was so much bright daylight, whether ten o'clock or even midnight.

After a few more days of travel along the Matanuska Mountain range we reached Eagle Trail State Park. There, we found a space big enough for both our RVs. We were getting settled and ready for a cookout when we heard quite a commotion outside. The people in the campsite next to ours were just starting to barbecue a salmon on their outdoor cooker when a black bear arrived and proceeded to take over. Needless to say, the ones preparing the meal lost no time getting into their rig. Alan grabbed his camcorder, thinking he'd get a picture of the action, but the bear thought otherwise; no one was going to get in his way, so Alan exited the scene in a hurry. No picture.

From inside our rig we watched that bear eat every bit of the salmon and knock the cooker off the table. After he'd eaten everything he could find, he tarried a while sniffing around to see if he could find anything more, and when he didn't, he added insult to injury by doing what comes naturally, and then ambling off into the woods.

Several more days of travel brought us to Haines, Alaska, which would be the starting point of our homeward journey. We had seen herds of wild horses, driven though hub-deep water where the nearby Chilkat River had flooded, visited Million Dollar Falls, and now looked forward to a few days of rest before we would board a working ferry southward bound.

Even though we were beginning to think of home, we still had many days of sights and experiences to encounter. We made our headquarters in the state park near Haines to await our scheduled time of departure. It was a good time to relax, also catch up on our housecleaning, laundry, etc. We went for hikes, one day through dense forest, over moss-covered logs and little brooks where masses of ferns grew profusely. We saw mushrooms of all sizes and shapes, brightly colored lichens clinging to the sides of dead trees, and so many plants that I would certainly call this the forest primeval.

Another day we walked to the water, this being the Lynn Canal. On the way, we stopped at the Visitors Center where we learned about the native plants and geography of the area. As we peered through the center's telescopes, observing Rainbow Glacier, we saw a huge piece of the glacier break off and fall and heard the resounding roar it made as it crashed into the water. We were told that the glacier was six or seven miles from where we were viewing it, and that we were fortunate to have seen the event, known as "calving," which happens infrequently.

That was the thrill for the day, we thought, as we left the center and meandered down to the water and out onto a pier just as a fisherman happened to be docking his boat and unloading his catch. Seeing Alan nearby, the fisherman summoned him closer and gave him a twenty-four-inch salmon, saying he had caught more than his limit. What a prize! We hurried back to our RVs and began preparing for a feast. Alan was "head chef," Margie and I contributed our portion, and Kenneth was on cleanup detail.

The next day we attended a fair in Haines. It was fun seeing the pig races, something I'd heard about but had never seen. There were also sled dog races. At this time of the year, with no snow, the sleds had wheels instead of runners, but it was interesting nonetheless. We watched the Klinget Indian dancers perform in native costume, and enjoyed seeing many interesting exhibits. We consumed a lot of fresh halibut and chips during this time. It was so good! There was a demonstration of Eskimo Indian Olympic Games and then the Sitka Indians performed their ceremonial dances, a very impressive sight. So ended another exciting day in Alaska.

On August 14, 1992, the day of departure arrived. We boarded the Alaskan ferry Malaspina at about 9:30 P.M. We had a cabin with two sets of bunk beds and a small bathroom — not exactly a luxury liner, but sufficient for our needs. The ferry carried a limited number of passengers and our vehicles. We spent the next two days leisurely viewing the scenery, listening to the interpreter, watching videos, and, of course, eating in the spacious dining room. It was too cold and windy to be out on the deck. When the ferry docked at Sitka, Alan and Margie got off and took a tour of the town. At Wrangel, we all left the boat and went ashore. There, we found youngsters on the dock selling garnets which are dug out of the ground in that vicinity. Many young people earn money for a college education this way. Later, when the boat stopped at Ketchikan, we again got off and walked a mile or so to the center of town, quite a fascinating place, built in the hills and along the waterfront. This town is accessible only by plane or boat.

On August 17 we reached the end of our ferry ride, driving off the boat at about 6:00 A.M., passing smoothly through customs, and into Prince Rupert, British Columbia. After another day's drive, we camped in a provincial park near the city of Prince George, British Columbia, and the next morning we toured a huge pulp mill. We were fascinated with the papermaking process, beginning with wood chips delivered by truck.

The following day we reached the U.S. border, crossed into Washington, camped a few more times, visited the brewery at Olympia, Washington, Pikes Market in Seattle, another fair in Lynden, Washington, and turned onto Highway 5, the final leg of our trip.

We reached Glen Ellen — home, sweet home! — on August 24th, 1992. It was the end of a wonderful, beautiful, spectacular, never-to-be-forgotten vacation.

Trip to Israel

During the 1990s, I took a winter trip to Israel, and it was an incredible experience. It is perhaps cliche to say that it made the *Bible* come alive, but indeed it did. Being an outdoor girl who loves nature, I especially enjoyed

Middle East Camel Ride. *Riding a camel was not the most comfortable of experiences, but it made my trip to Israel more memorable.*

our time on the Sea of Galilee. It was an awesome experience to stand on the Mount of the Beatitudes and gaze out upon the Sea of Galilee and the surrounding mountains and hear Matthew 6, 7 and 8 read aloud. There were even wildflowers and birds to enhance the scene. Seated on a boat in the middle of the sea was equally exciting. Now, when I study the *Bible* I have a realistic vision of Christ's ministry around the Sea of Galilee.

I also appreciated our hike in Ein Gedi to see the area where David hid in the cave and had the opportunity to slay Saul, but didn't.

Pastor Chris Bower's Saturday morning classes the month prior to our departure were invaluable. Having prior knowledge and insights about what we were going to see greatly enhanced the trip.

I recommend that anyone considering a trip to Israel, go! You won't read God's Word quite the same again.

Down Mexico Way

After learning about another tour named "Fantasy Caravan," it sounded interesting to Kenneth and me, so we joined my son, Alan, and his wife, Margie, in our respective travel vehicles for the forty-two-day trip to Mexico, leaving home on February 1, 1995. Four days of travel brought us to Nogales, Arizona, where we met the others in the tour group.

We were tagged officially with numbers on the vehicles and name tags on our person, and given information about traffic, customs, etc. in Mexico. The next day the caravan — fourteen vehicles with fifty passengers — crossed the border into Mexico, proceeding to our first destination, Guaymas, on the Sea of Cortez, where we spent the rest of that day sightseeing, bedded down that night at a bright, clean RV park, and went sightseeing again the next day.

The following morning found the caravan on the road to the next town and camp. Many different kinds of flowers were growing everywhere. In the little town of Alamos, we walked the cobblestone streets, visited a local house built of adobe walls three feet thick with fireplaces in every room and a beautiful courtyard surrounded by a high wall. The walking tour took us farther on to another area where houses were not so elegant, and a variety of animals wandered around —household pets, chickens, even a few pigs and goats. Every house seemed to have dogs, some looking half starved, strolling in and out of open doors.

Our next stop was the little town of Mochis, where we were given a train trip into the awe-inspiring Copper Canyon. The train left at 7 P.M. and for eight hours climbed and wound around extremely mountainous terrain, once making a complete 180-degree switchback or an "S" curve. The scenery was simply incredible, trees with gorgeous pink blossoms, others with huge yellow flowers. These, we were told, were kapok trees. We soon reached the town of Creel where we spent the night and the next day. There, we visited the cave-dwelling Indians. We witnessed poverty in the extreme, people living in caves, and I wondered how they survived. There was a mission in the area, and a school, which we visited.

Our bus stopped by a beautiful lake, and then took us back to the hotel in Creel where we spent the night. We boarded the train next morning to return to Mochis. The coach was old and the dirtiest I had ever seen.

The next day, after driving all day over rough roads, we arrived in Mazatlan where our RV park was in a coconut grove. Over a period of several days, we took a side trip to Stone Island, rowed in small boats across the harbor, then debarked and took a small local taxi to the other side of the island, which is in the Sea of Cortez. Late in the afternoon we again rode the little taxi back to the pier, taking the boat back to our cars. That evening we attended a Mexican fiesta at the large Hotel Playa. The food was good and the show excellent.

Leaving Mazatlan, the caravan made its way to San Blas and the RV park. That night we enjoyed a pot luck supper with the rest of the members of the caravan. It was a great meal, and birthdays and anniversaries were celebrated with a cake.

After lunch the next day, we carpooled to a nearby honest-to-goodness jungle where we enjoyed a fascinating boat ride. As we drifted along a swamp stream that wound through dense tropical foliage and hanging vines, we saw colorful tropical birds in lush green trees, turtles dodging and swimming away from our boat, even a small crocodile slithering into the water. It was exciting, but a bit scary, too. When we arrived back at camp, we were hot, sweaty and tired ... and filled with satisfaction after our wonderful jungle experience.

After a restful night's sleep, we were up early, eager for our next adventure. We drove along winding, hilly roads through fertile farm land, banana and papaya groves, and acres and acres of tobacco fields. We also passed through several small villages where our caravan caused much interest. The children especially waved and smiled enthusiastically and, of course, we loved waving to them, too. We reached the town of Rincon De Guayabitos by the middle of the morning and spent considerable time getting parked. Some members of our caravan were parked on one side of town; the rest, on the other side. We spent the next several days here, relaxing and resting.

Our RV park was close to the beach, so we were able to do a bit of swimming. One afternoon, all of the caravaners were given rides in glass bottom boats out to and circling an island in the bay. The water was so clear that the many colorful fish swimming in the water were clearly visible.

In a few more days, driving many miles through numerous small villages and observing groves of exotic fruit, we camped in the RV park at the little village of Chimulco, on the site of an ancient volcano. Its many pools are fed by hot springs, and everyone enjoyed bathing in the natural hot water.

The next morning we were taken to see a very unusual sight created by one man, a Señor Garcia, who was eighty-five years old at the time of our visit. Over a period of fifty-eight years, using only a pick, shovel, and his burro for hauling dirt, he had dug into a good-sized hill to create a huge cave, into which he had built a church. The ceiling was arched, twelve- to fifteen-feet high, all finished with textured plaster made from material he had moved. In order to have light in the dark cave, he had strategically placed a mirror, which was approximately two-and-a-half feet by one-and-a-half feet, to catch and reflect the sun. He demonstrated this to us by casting the reflection onto the altar. The light was brighter than a spotlight. Señor Garcia began digging in 1939 and fifty-eight years later, when we were there in 1997, he was still in good health and adding the finishing tiles.

Several days later, having driven countless miles and visiting a glass factory, a huge pottery operation and a furniture construction site, we reached the next RV camp near the City of Guadalajara, Mexico. Our entire party boarded a tour bus that took us to downtown Guadalajara. We entered the huge Cathedral and were awed by its beauty and magnificent architecture, the lofty marble arches edged in gold, countless marble statues of saints, numerous stained glass windows, and a bright white marble floor. There happened to be a service, or mass, being conducted at this time, so we exited the cathedral and made our way to the nearby opera house, another impressive building. Here again, there was opulence in the building's size and interior furnishings and decorations, having five tiers of balconies and box seats. We were seated on the main floor, where we witnessed a thrilling performance, the Ballet Folklorico. For two full hours we were treated to grand and enthralling entertainment featuring talented performers in gorgeous costumes singing and dancing to music that was beautiful and exciting.

After several days of rest, we were ready to move on. With the help of the Green Angels (comparable to our State Highway Patrol) and directions provided by our Wagon Master, we were able to get onto the freeway. Then, by staying as close together as possible, we made it through Guadalajara fairly smoothly, and we were soon on the mountainous, two-lane road to Zacatecas, Mexico.

From our RV camp, we carpooled to Zacatecas, a city of 450,000. First, we went inside the Basilic Cathedral and noted the usual richness of the Catholic Church. Then, we went to the building that holds the Pedro Coronel Museum where we were impressed with the collections of books dating back centuries and rooms filled with paintings by famous artists Dali, Goya, Picasso, and many more. One room contained masks of every kind; another room, sculptures, many dating back many centuries before Christ.

While most of our group were admiring the paintings, one of our fellow travelers stepped outside the room to wait for us, and he accidentally brushed against a ladder, causing it to move against a large display case, which came crashing down, scattering glass everywhere and causing a great deal of consternation among the guards and officials of the museum. The display case contained valuable paintings which lost most of their glass. The resolution of this unfortunate accident caused quite a delay for us.

On this last day of our tour, we left Zacatecas and traveled to Saltillo. On the way there our vehicle began having engine trouble, and others were also experiencing trouble. Our "tail gunner," the mechanic, used his expertise and we arrived in Saltillo for our final party. We were both happy and sad, for this ended forty-two fun-filled days with Fantasy Caravan. With fond farewells, we bid adieus to the good friends we had met along the way.

Desert Dilemma

For many years Kenneth and I made a yearly trek to Colorado and Kansas for a combined pleasure and business trip. He had a farm in Kansas and his family was there and in Colorado. Sometimes we flew, but mostly we traveled by automobile.

In the summer of 1997 we traveled in our motor home, always a pleasurable mode of transportation for us. Kenneth's favorite route was Interstate Highway 50, which I always thought boring and lonely because towns were few and far between with vast stretches of desert through Nevada and Utah. But the road was good and traffic was light, which pleased Kenneth.

By evening of our first day we had reached Fallon, Nevada, and camped in a very nice motor park. All was well as we began the second day and passed through the little town of Austin, Nevada, the last bit of civilization we would see for the next hundred or more miles. We were somewhere in the middle of the desert when the motor home's engine quietly died, leaving us coasting to a wide spot alongside the road. We tried contacting the Highway Patrol with our CB, but we were too far away to get a signal.

The only solution to our dilemma was to flag down a motorist and, thankfully, Highway 50 is frequented by commercial truckers. We had a windshield protector in the RV, a large cardboard which folded when not in use. On one side, printed in big letters, were the words, "Help! Call Police." Kenneth stood at the edge of the road with the sign held high. In a short time a large truck appeared, the driver stopped and, after hearing about our plight, promised to contact the Highway Patrol, who would come to our rescue.

Having sent our SOS, there was little we could do but wait, so I prepared lunch and afterward we brought out the games we carried with us. No need to fret or worry when reading materials or games are available. Hours later, as we began to wonder if the truck driver had really delivered our call for help, a state patrol officer pulled up behind our rig, and soon a tow truck was there to haul us back to a garage in Fallon, a distance of at least 150 miles. Now we knew why this highway was called the loneliest road in the U.S.A.

Seeing Versus Hearing

There are numerous quips concerning sight, such as "what you see is what you get" and "seeing is believing," but what about hearing? If there are any out there, I haven't heard them or don't remember any. In my opinion,

Celebrating Nine Decades, 2006. *For my nintieth birthday, my children and grandchildren created a collage of photos from my past, representative of the many phases of my life.*

there should be.

As a case in point, I am reminded of a brief conversation between my husband, Kenneth, and a female acquaintance. It took place on a Sunday morning around 2000, and we had just entered the narthex of our church. We were greeted warmly by many, and as we had arrived a bit early, there was ample time for considerable visiting and small talk.

A most attractive middle-aged lady whom Kenneth and I had known for a long time approached us and, after the usual handshake and welcome, she asked Kenneth, "Are you going to go for a cold beer?" At least, that is what I thought she said.

Kenneth discretely replied, "No, I don't think so."

I seriously doubted whether Kenneth even knew what beer tasted like, having been raised by a family who strictly forbade the consumption of anything stronger than coffee.

The morning service was about to begin, so Kenneth and I made our way down the aisle and seated ourselves in a pew. Soon, the sanctuary grew quiet as people prepared for worship. In those moments of silence, my thoughts were not of a spiritual nature, however; I kept thinking about the strange question our friend had asked my husband. It was so out of character for her, timewise as well as personally.

My revelation was soon to come when a church member arose to make announcements of coming events. Plans were underway, he said, for "Western Night," an annual program at our church. Among other things the speaker reminded us about the beard-growing contest for men in the congregation.

Suddenly, the light clicked on in my brain, and I realized that the question our friend had asked Kenneth was, "Are you going to grow a beard?"

So, things may not always be what they seem to be on sight, but they certainly can be quite different in hearing, too. Especially when one reaches the age of Social Security and Medicare, and hearing is about fifty percent gone.

Farewell to Summer

The autumn has always given me a feeling of some sadness. The summer flowers are spent and dying, the days are growing shorter, and with each passing night there is a little more chill in the air, with the promise of more to come. This year as I clean the leaves and other debris from my garden there is more than a little sadness in my heart. In the center of one raised bed stands a very dear little church building, a prized possession which has graced our garden decor for many years. Having withstood winter rains and summer's scorching rays, it has finally succumbed and is now in a state of disrepair, literally falling apart. So, like the words of the song "This Old House," it's also "ready to meet the saints."

As a bit of explanation, it wasn't always a church building. When Kenneth and I married in 1980, a friend gave us a beautiful little kitten. It was about half grown, and Kenneth thought the cat should have a house of its own, rather than live in our house. He loved building things, so this was a fun project for him. The proportions were approximately twenty inches by twenty-four inches, with a pitched roof, windows with glass panes, and a door. Kenneth even papered the interior with some pretty wallpaper, brushed a coat of white paint on the small structure and added a green roof. The final crowning touch was painting the cat's name — SAM — above the door.

We found that we weren't exactly knowledgeable regarding feline foibles when we introduced Sam to his luxurious abode. One look at it and he took off running, expressing some sort of cat expletive as he went. I interpreted it as "No way are you going to get me cooped up in that miserable little cage." He opted instead for sleeping quarters in the garage. And the cat's little house sat on the patio, more or less unnoticed except for the infrequent times a small granddaughter briefly played house with her dolls there.

Glorious Days in Our Glen Ellen Garden. *Kenneth and I enjoyed working with our hands — crafting objects and also growing flowers, fruit and vegetables in Glen Ellen, California. Shown above left, Kenneth holds giant onions with more in the cart in front of him, and I, on the right, prepare to weigh an enormous head of cabbage on a bathroom scale.*

Kenneth and I both enjoyed creating things with our hands, such as crafts and artistic objects. One day I suggested to him that we make the cat's little house into a replica of the church we attended, which was just down the street from our home. Kenneth's little structure already had the same simple lines of architecture. All it needed was a new front entry, a bell tower, and some stained glass windows. Kenneth liked the idea, so we got busy. He built the bell tower and steps leading up to the Gothic-style front door he'd designed. I gathered different pieces of colored glass and glued every small segment of the varied colors to the existing glass in the windows. From my store of trinkets I found a tiny bell just the right size for the bell tower. A fresh coat of paint soon covered Sam's name over the front door, and we looked with pleasure upon our almost perfect replica of the little church on O'Donnell Lane in Glen Ellen.

From that time until the present, our miniature church has occupied a prominent place in our garden, from Glen Ellen to Healdsburg, where we moved in 1999 and where I still live. In the past, at Christmas time it was surrounded by a small village composed of little buildings, also made by Kenneth, all of them aglow with lights. Kenneth's forte was decorating at Christmastime, and he made our home in Glen Ellen a showplace every holiday season. The whole community knew and enjoyed our decorations, as well as our hospitality.

So it is with a heavy heart, doubly so because Kenneth is no longer with me, that I now must retire our little church building, which was so dear and lovely in its day but is now old and collapsing into oblivion. A few years after celebrating the turn of the new century, both Kenneth and I began to experience health problems. His condition was so severe that he required professional care and was moved to a nursing facility far away from me. Sadly, he passed away on November 1, 2008, leaving me with only precious memories of our happy days together.

CHAPTER FIVE

2007 — and Beyond
LOVE & LAUGHTER

After losing my dear Kenneth, I once again made a conscious decision to move forward. Trusting in God to guide me, I considered all the blessings in my life: My health had improved, my family and friends were caring and helpful, my church was spiritually enriching, my writers group provided creative support for my work, and I could still drive. So, I stepped into the ninth decade of my life with optimism, and the ensuing years have been filled with many accomplishments and, more important, an abundance of love and laughter.

Grandma Comes Out of the Closet

What a revelation! Never be too certain of one's convictions. Yesterday's doubts may become today's certainties ... or, perhaps, only an illusion.

A few years ago my son-in-law, Joe McBurney, came calling on me to ascertain if I needed help starting my car. When he received no response to a short ring of the doorbell, he used the house key, which he always carries with him, and entered the living room. Not finding me there, he began to search from room to room — kitchen, dining room, family room, and bedrooms. When he failed to find me at the computer in my "studio" (so named because I enjoy art work and sewing there in addition to computer work), he felt certain he'd find me in the backyard tending my garden. Alas, there was no sign of the old girl there either. That left only the garage; if the car was gone, that would account for my absence. But when Joe opened the door to the garage, there sat the car! The mystery deepened by the minute. He had previously noted my jacket and purse in their usual place and he knew that I never go anywhere without them.

As Joe's concern reached a new level, he headed for the telephone in the kitchen, and while he pondered the situation, trying to decide whether to call the police, the neighbors or my mother, who should suddenly appear but his mother-in-law — ME — in the flesh, startling the daylights out of him, not to mention what suddenly seeing him did to me. Due to my hearing deficit, I had not heard the doorbell, nor footsteps on the carpeted floor. And, of course, my cat doesn't bark, and heads for his hiding place when anyone comes.

"Where WERE you?" Joe asked with some consternation. "I searched everywhere for you, thought you'd been abducted or something."

"I was in the closet of my studio," I answered, "looking for some documents that I want to shred. I had stored them in the chest of drawers there, and it took a little while to find them."

Nerves soon settled down after Grandma came out of the closet.

Pins and Needles Retirement

With the help of my mother and sewing classes in school, I learned to make my own clothes during my youth. After Alan and Gretchan were born, I really went into high gear, sewing clothes for both my children as well as myself. I especially enjoyed making Gretchan's feminine clothes, with my favorite creation being her wedding dress. Hers was the third wedding dress I had made, the first being my wedding dress and second, the dress I stitched for my daughter-in-law, Margie.

Many years later I also had the satisfaction of creating wedding gowns for our family's younger generation — for my two beautiful granddaughters, Heather Huffman and Laura McBurney. I was content, feeling that I had brought my sewing career full circle. So, I have hung up my scissors, put away the pins and needles, and retired. No more wedding dresses ... at least not dresses that I sewed.

Revisiting the House on O'Donnell Lane

I had been living in Healdsburg for almost ten years when a telephone call reminded me of the differences people have in tastes and ideas, which, of course, is usually a good thing. What a dull world it would be if everyone thought alike. However, sometimes those differences can be painful.

The call was from a friend who had been my nearest neighbor when I lived in Glen Ellen, and after I moved, we continued to maintain contact by telephone when we couldn't get together in person. When making a reference to my former home in Glen Ellen, she always referred to it as "my house," as though my family still owned it.

There was a time when I firmly believed that I would never leave that house, so much of my very being went into the building of it, and so many years spent working together to accomplish Byron's and my goals and dreams. But time brings change. When my children grew up and created separate families, and my life's partner passed away, my home no longer filled me with peace and joy as it once had. I believe the final blow to my heart came when the gigantic oak tree that had shaded the patio for many years became diseased and had to be taken down.

On the day my former neighbor called, she said, "Did you know your house is for sale? Would you like to buy it back?"

I thought of my reasons for leaving there and told her that I was not the least bit interested in moving back. I had moved on with my life, and besides, it wasn't the same house. The new owners had made many changes to the property, erasing the personality of "my house." Before they were even settled in, they removed the approximately thirty-foot flagpole in the front yard that had been a real source of pride for Byron and me. Next came the demise of three small shrubs that I had spent years training into bonsai sculptures. Then I guess it was time for the new owners to start remodeling the house, for the brick that came out of the kiln on the property, and enhanced the house with lovely mellowed charm, came down and was hauled to the dump. I couldn't believe anyone would cut the big redwood trees that grew on the back of the property, but they did. We had planted the trees when they were fifteen inches, and they had reached a height of forty feet

Up until the time I left, the very thought of leaving the house on O'Donnell Lane was agonizing. It meant leaving behind all that had formed and shaped the foundation of four decades of my family's life. But life is filled with changes, and my new home would become a source of progression, opening a new chapter in my life. Moving back to Glen Ellen and to the house on O'Donnell Lane could never be the same.

Facing Forty

When my last grandchild recently celebrated the fortieth year of her birth, I was reminded of my own fortieth birthday, which was less than joyous. I was in no mood to glibly accept the old saw, "life begins at forty." In fact, my attitude was one of discouragement, skepticism and doubt, rather than joy and thankfulness as it should have been.

Byron had invited a couple to join us for dinner to celebrate the special occasion, and the evening went well. However, it was all I could do to hide my true feeling — depression. Forty sounded so old to me! Fortunately, in a day or two I realized that life would go on, and my attitude changed to one of hope. I realize now that it was God speaking to me. What a revelation!

Not long after that milestone birthday, a number of new and exciting things came my way: a wonderful job and the discovery that I could paint, carve figures, and create clay models. What joy these newfound abilities brought to me ... and continue to bring. I came to realize that each newly discovered talent was a gift from God.

All the Days of My Life

Most people who live as long as I have are often asked about their longevity, that is, to what do we attribute it. First and foremost, I believe that I inherited good genes. My grandfather John Dietz Younkin lived into his ninety-fifth year; my father, John King Younkin, into his eightieth year; and my mother, Edna Younkin, into her eighty-seventh year. Although many of my brothers and sisters died young, due to the lack of immunizations and antibiotics during that era, two of my brothers, Clarence and Chet, survived into their seventies, Harold reached age ninety five, and Paul and I are in our nineties.

I have always eaten a healthy diet, but nothing out of the ordinary, and I still exercise regularly — walking and working in my garden. However, I'm not sure whether those things have added to my years or if inherited good health at my advanced age simply makes physical activity enjoyable.

Helping others, remaining as independent as possible, and tackling projects that are mentally stimulating are important to a full and happy life at any age. I also think it's important to communicate regularly with younger people, listening to and discussing the interests of children, grandchildren, great-grandchildren, and others of the younger set. You never know how you might be inspired. Recently, I watched one of my great-grandchildren riding a new bicycle and I had an incredible urge to give it a try. I didn't, but just imagining the experience made me feel like a kid again.

I believe it is important to have a positive outlook on life and during hard times trust that things will eventually improve. Worrying about things one cannot change accomplishes nothing useful and adds more stress to one's body, mind and spirit, which is very unhealthy.

The Future

I don't know what God has planned for my future, but I believe it will be good. Every day when I wake up, I take a deep breath and count my blessings, which are many. Happiness, optimism and confidence fill me, and I am inspired to accomplish whatever I can in the years ahead. I plan to continue my usual daily routine — keeping house, gardening, cooking, and exercising — with time left over to cuddle my cat, Joey. I look forward to church services and gathering with family and friends for special meals and events. I'll undoubtedly write more stories, but my main goal is to once again spend happy hours painting pictures and playing the piano, both of which I've neglected while working on this book.

Since the day of my birth in 1916, my life has been one adventure after another, and I feel certain it will continue to be wonderful and exciting. At ninety-six years of age, I still have things to do and places to go, and it is with eager anticipation that I once again step into an unknown but promising future.

Faithful Friends. *Joey is a handsome, clever and loving companion who enriches my life. When he snuggles up to me and purrs, peace and joy fill my heart.*

❤ ❤ ❤

"She is clothed with strength and honor ... When she speaks, her words are wise ... Her children stand and bless her."
Proverbs 31:25-28

SURNAME INDEX

Note: Married surnames are in parentheses

SURNAME INDEX

BIBLIOGRAPHY & RESOURCES

Biographical History of Barton County, Kansas, Great Bend Tribune, Great Bend, Kansas, 1912

First Methodist Church, Great Bend, Kansas, Photo Archives

History of Washington and Ozaukee Counties, Wisconsin, Western Historical Co., Chicago, Illinois, 1881

Younkin, John Dietz (1837-1932), handwritten autobiography

TO ORDER . . .

To order *Marietta's Stories: From Kansas to California, Memories of My Life* by mail, please complete this order form and forward with check, money order or credit card information to Rayve Productions, POB 726, Windsor CA 95492. If paying with a credit card, you can call us toll-free at 800.852.4890 or fax this completed form to Rayve Productions at 707.838.2220.

We invite you to visit the Rayve Productions website and view our books at rayveproductions.com.

❏ Please send me the following book(s):

Title _*Marietta's Stories*_   Price $ _24.95_ Qty ___ Amount $ _____

Title _____   Price _____ Qty ___ Amount $ _____

Subtotal	$ _____

**Quantity Discount: 4 items -10%;
10 items -15%; 25 items -20%**

Sales Tax: Californians please add 8% sales tax
Shipping & Handling:
Media Mail — $3.99 for first book + $2 each additional
Priority Mail — $5.50 for first book + $2 each additional

Subtotal $ _____
Discount $ _____
Shipping $ _____
Subtotal $ _____
Sales Tax $ _____
Total $ _____

Name _____   Phone _____ — _____
                                                                          Area Code
Address _____

City State Zip _____

❏ Check enclosed $ _____

❏ Charge my Visa/MC $ _____

Credit card # _____   Exp. Date _____

Signature _____

Thank you!